DIARY OF A CHRISTIAN SINGLE

FLYING
Solo

Käaren Witte

Abingdon Press

Nashville

Flying Solo: Diary of a Christian Single

Copyright © 1988 by Abingdon Press

All rights reserved.
No part of this work may be reproduced or transmitted in any form or by any means, electronic or mechanical, including photocopying and recording, or by any information storage or retrieval system, except as may be expressly permitted by the 1976 Copyright Act or in writing from the publisher. Requests for permission should be addressed in writing to Abingdon Press, 201 Eighth Avenue South, Nashville, TN 37202.

This book is printed on acid-free paper.

Library of Congress Cataloging-in-Publication Data
WITTE, KÄAREN.
 Flying solo.
 1. Witte, Käaren. 2. Christian biography—United States. 3. Single women—United States—Biography.
 I. Title.
 BR1725.W57A3   1988   248.8'432   87-33689
 ISBN 0-687-13250-9 (alk. paper)

ISBN 0-687-13250-9

"Forgive Me Jesus. Again," text pp. 38-40, originally printed under the title "I Forgive, in the Name of Jesus" in *Aglow*, January–February 1981, and reprinted with permission.

"Easy Rider and Me," text pp. 46-50, reprinted from *Aglow*, September–October 1981, with permission.

"How to Be Beautiful Without Being Good Looking," text pp. 121-28, reprinted from *Christian Single,* March 1985. © copyright 1985 The Sunday School Board of the Southern Baptist Convention. All rights reserved. Used by permission of the author.

Text on p. 130 taken from January 1984 issue of *The Daily Walk*. Copyright 1984, Walk Thru the Bible Ministries, Inc., Atlanta, GA. Used by permission.

Scripture quotation marked TLB is from the *Modern Language Bible: The Berkely Version in Modern English*. Copyright © 1945, 1959, 1969 by Zondervan Publishing House. Used by permission.

Scripture quotation marked NIV taken from the *Holy Bible: New International Version*. Copyright © 1973, 1978, 1984 by the International Bible Society. Used by permission of Zondervan Bible Publishers.

Excerpt from *Love Must Be Tough* by James Dobson, copyright © 1983 by Word Books. Used by permission.

MANUFACTURED BY THE PARTHENON PRESS AT
NASHVILLE, TENNESSEE, UNITED STATES OF AMERICA

To Al Witte, my father

Whom I asked when I was three years old, "Daddy, are you God?"
He always represented God to me and our family.
He has stirred more emotion and commanded more respect than any man I have known in my lifetime.

To my late mother, Lilly Nelson Witte

She loved me.
She left the door open and the light on so I could see my way up.

To Hazel Witte

After all these years
I still would pick her for Mom II.

Acknowledgments

Prince Charles   I forgive you.

**The Reverend
Doug Burr**   A man who believed in me during dark days and kept affirming me with "You're going to take the world!"

Ruthe Lamb   She continually says, "You singles are my whole life, my family."
She loves us like her own.
She has no fear of old age or anything else.

Jan Markell   A real friend to me.
She keeps forgiving me.

A gracious thank you to those whose thoughts from sermons, conversations, and tapes have found their way into my heart and vocabulary.

Foreword

I have never forgotten the single adult who came up to me after I had spoken on singleness and celibacy. "But I'm tired of being good," she announced. Among some single adults, the notion is that if one is "good" then one gets a reward for singleness: a mate. Others think of singleness as a prison sentence, and they expect time off for their good behavior.

There are many ways to play the waiting game. Unfortunately, negative attitudes keep many single adults from experiencing the best of singleness. In too many, the hurt turns into resentment and eventually cynical rebellion. Individuals become no longer single for a season but single for a reason.

That's not true of Käaren Witte. A single woman, never married, over thirty, Käaren wants to marry. And she's deliberate about analyzing the claims of those who stalk the countryside on white chargers (or in metallic blue Trans Ams) claiming to be Prince Charming.

Käaren is waiting, as are thousands of other women.

Waiting is no fun for those single adults who want to be married. Who want to be loved. Who want to be held. Who want to translate a thousand hopes and dreams into memories. The enemy would offer such single adults discounts, bargains, or counterfeits.

Käaren has *chosen* to wait with class. She invests herself in the lives of others: whether a Hell's Angel motorcyclist or an Israeli child.

That's an incredible model.

I have long believed that singleness is either a problem or an opportunity. Every single adult has to decide which it will be. Käaren's message is that it can be a tremendous string of opportunities. Her words will help you make the decision to find the opportunities in your singleness. And it just may be what you need to switch your perspective.

Does God have a mate picked out for you? I cannot speak for God on that point. I *can* say that he has not promised us marriage, but he has promised himself. And many single adults have found that special grace while waiting: the gift of his Son. "His divine power has given us everything we need for life and godliness" (II Peter 1:3 NIV).

Käaren Witte will help you understand that gift of waiting.

Harold Ivan Smith

Contents

    Introduction..13
I. Dreams and Visions...15
II. Questions...83
III. My Soul Sings... 139

Introduction

I'm over thirty.
Never married.
I am a woman.
I wait.
Do you wait with me?
I believe. I trust.
Do you?
I know you do.
God speaks to me in tones only the single can understand.
You understand.
One reader of *Great Leaps in a Single Bound* insisted, when my publisher handed her a copy of the book, "And I suppose at the end Käaren Witte married and lived happily ever after."
I can't tell you that. What I can tell you is that I am a single woman with the same longings, hopes, and desires as any woman who ever lived and dreamed.
I *can* tell you there will be enough grace for you. Each day. Each moment. Each year. Each time you cry.
I want you to believe in the God who has carried me this far.
I want to tell you, "Look! I waited and God gave me this wonderful mate for my life, who is loving me like no woman has ever been loved before. And if you follow Christ and believe, he will do the same for you."
But I can't.

I don't know what he will do with your life. I don't know what assignments he will give you. I don't know when he will fulfill his promises to you.
But he will.
Sometime.
Someplace.
Somehow.
Some way. Always.
I do know *I am you*. That's why I love you so desperately.
I know your hurt, your pain. (Also your freedom.)
You are the *we* of *me*.

Dreams and Visions

1

Fall 1979

Please Believe in Me

Lucille. We called her an old maid. She was between thirty-five and forty. We were teenagers at summer camp. In fact, at my wilderness summer camp there were so many unmarried counselors we teens joked that camp was "virgin territory."

I loved camp. I was an insignificant kid, growing up. I was so socially stunted that I would hide when I saw kids from school. (If they can't see me, they can't have the option of rejecting me, I decided.)

But at camp we were all Christians, and we loved one another. The other kids thought I was fun. And funny. I knew I was accepted and in ten years as a camper I hardly remember walking from one building to another without being arm in arm with somebody. At the closing campfire each year we sobbed at parting.

Hundreds of us teens had grown up together at camp; we were pals. Buddies. Our days teemed with singing, hugs, swimming, and girltalk about future husbands. (Carolyn had a boyfriend in the summer of '66. She was a high school senior. He was a college man—a football player. Since the previous summer she had lost twenty-five pounds. She was a size six and wore madras blouses. We dreamed too.)

I wasn't brilliant in school. I wasn't brilliant at camp, either. I never won many awards or trophies. But it didn't matter too much. Because at camp I was loved.

Except I knew I wasn't loved by Lucille.

Nobody felt loved by her. But her cold, icy personality

never thwarted us from coming to camp. Surely we could tolerate a legalistic attitude and a constipated face!

Lucille was an authority figure at the camp and a secretary during the school year. How I wanted her approval! Whenever I committed some indiscriminate or stupid deed, I would inevitably be caught by her. (Even in those early days of my Christian pilgrimage, I understood God. I knew his friendship and compassion. Even though Lucille was an authority figure—a Christian leader—I didn't blur the two! I still knew Friend Jesus thought we teens were cute, funny, and adorable. And she couldn't change his mind.)

I remember cutting another girl's hair in the dishwashing room one night. "Oh, no! What rotten timing!" I gasped, as I snipped Jeannie's long blond hair. "Here comes Lucille!"

Jeannie's eyes burned in mine. There was no time to run. (It was only at that moment that our young adolescent wisdom told us that we shouldn't have been engaged in haircutting in the dishwashing room.)

"What do you think this is? What are you two doing cutting hair *in here?* Don't you have common sense?" Lucille lashed.

Jeannie jumped up from the cup rack on which she was perched. Half of her hair was cut to shoulder length, the other half hung at her waist.

I grabbed a broom. Lucille raged, "This is unsanitary. Don't you have any breeding? And it is time for 'Taps.' You two are not going to be given the privilege of staying and working for boys' camp! I'll make sure of it. You've sealed your doom. Now get to your cabin!"

We exited. The screen door slammed.

"Those two are brainless and immature. They'll never amount to anything," Lucille ranted to the head cook, who popped in on the ugly scene.

Going out the door, we caught those words. We grabbed each other, stomped up the hill, and bawled. Throwing myself on my bunk bed, I moaned, "We won't get to stay for boys' camp next month." (Can you imagine the heady thrill? Teenage girls serving tables and doing dishes for three hundred boys?)

It's a funny thing. Stupid, I know, and psychologically weak. But I was never able to brush her off. I was haunted by Lucille's opinion of me.

But Lucille did have a special knack for finding four-leaf clovers. Bending down to a patch, she would flip through the greens and find one! I often commented to the other campers on her uncanny luck!

My pal Pam quickly insisted, "Käaren, if that's luck, let's hope we never find a four-leaf clover!"

We howled. And hugged. Nothing and nobody would change that.

In the summer of '66, I was the last lifeguard to leave the beach one afternoon. Lucille beckoned me to her.

Oh, no. Now what? I anguished mentally.

Was she plotting this? My mind raced as I walked to the bench. This wasn't her usual mode of instruction and discipline. She'd always made public with her "why-let-the-sins-of-one-be-wasted-let-everyone-profit" approach to dealing with teens.

"Sit down," she ordered. She paused and then questioned, "What are you going to do with your life?"

"I'm going to be a teacher. And I'd love to be married and have a family—ah, like most people." Then I gulped, realizing that she didn't.

"You won't make a teacher. And you girls, all you think about is having some man's shoes under your bed!" she snapped, slinging her towel around her neck.

As she jumped up and left, I sputtered something to redeem myself. But she didn't hear.

"I don't *only* think about getting married—I've only accepted a few dates in my life," I called to her back and the wind.

Am I really such an awful girl? I interrogated myself. Her words "brainless" and "immature" slammed me again, as I continued to beat myself emotionally. Cool tears flushed down my deeply tanned face. *Why doesn't she see my good* qualities? Maybe I don't have any. Maybe my friends and the other loving, laughing leaders are wrong. Maybe she's the only one who sees the real me.

"Are you in trouble? What did Lucille say to you? I saw you talking to her down at the beach. It looked serious," Roseanne, one of my pals, pressed me back at the cabin.

"Lucille . . . She doesn't believe in me. Why doesn't she like me, Roseanne?" I begged.

"What did she say?" Roseanne asked.

"I can't tell you. It hurts too much." I sobbed in Roseanne's arms. Mentally, I determined that if I told Roseanne, she might believe Lucille. I couldn't risk it. Not at that moment.

Years have passed. Now I'm in the safety of adulthood. But why do I feel so strongly about Lucille, to this day?

A few years ago my dad was volunteering at camp. Lucille was still working with teens. My first book, *Angels in Faded Jeans*, had been published.

"Dad! Did you give Lucille a copy? I hope so! I want her above anyone in the world to see I wasn't the hopeless, immature, wayward, man-hungry teen she thought I was! Did you give her a copy and tell her about me? Did you?" I begged.

"No, honey. I didn't," he said, his voice lowered and his head bowed.

"I know. My motives are wrong, Dad. Rather than minister to her or bless her, I only wanted to show her," I confessed.

Later, while visiting the Wisconsin area, I returned to the campgrounds. I walked down the pebbled paths that led to clusters of cabins with romantic Indian names like Shawnee and Mohawk. I walked down to the waterfront. The beach was silent. No campers, whistles, or water sounds. Only the leaves rustled, now.

The moment had come.

I had returned to the place that had given me so much love. But I needed to forgive. And release. And be free.

I sank down on the very bench where I had sat with Lucille so many years before.

I remembered what Christ did for me.

Inside my purse I found the Saltine cracker package from a restaurant. I placed a piece on my tongue and whispered, "This is my body, broken for you."

I bent down and scooped lake water into my hand. Touching the water with my mouth and tongue, I whispered, "This is my blood which was shed for you."

I was free. New. I sobbed and shouted across the lake, "I forgive you, Lu-u-c-ille!"

A sobbing, broken voice echoed, "I forgive you . . ."

We have been forgiven by God far more than we'll ever need to forgive others.

Summer 1966

Watching

I grew up in a small town with a root beer stand and kids who dragged Main Street, radios blaring.

I struggled through childhood aware that I wasn't extraordinarily gifted or beautiful. In adolescence, I didn't dream. (What girl had the impetus even to aspire to broadcast journalism in Worthington, Minnesota, in 1966?)

The socially skilled child-stars in school won the teachers' hearts and one another's. The cheerleaders strutted, all sweaters and pleated skirts. They had boyfriends—tall, confident athletes.

So they *seemed* to me in 1966.

Those boyfriends winked and gabbed with the old lady teachers, who got giggly at the attention.

I just watched.

Fall 1968

A Prayer

Dear God,
 Give me the privilege of holding a dirty, dying Peruvian indian or an Ethiopian peasant with hair that smells bad and skin that is wrinkled and ulcerated.
 Let me have the privilege of ushering her into eternity as she invites Jesus Christ into her heart and dies coughing up blood, from tuberculosis.
 I have died to myself. One more time.
 It doesn't matter where I live, what I eat, or where I sleep.
 Give me a tough assignment in life, a job nobody wants. Amen.

P S. I don't want to be single, however.

Summer 1972

Where in the World Is Love?

Nice, France.
"Where is love? Will I ever know the sweet hello that's meant for only me?"

These words from the musical *Oliver!* surfaced from deep inside me, as I sat by the Mediterranean Sea. I was living in Nice, France. I was a student—sometimes.

Most days I walked only as far as the sea, the half-way point between my student housing and the campus. But even this bluest water in the world washed pain over me in its wake.

Even the animals live in pairs, I thought, watching birds picking their food on the beach.

There's a person alone, I continued thinking, *but he's a derelict.* The temperature was eighty degrees, but he was wearing a baggy winter coat and shoes without socks.

Why had I left my little apartment above the tree level? Third floor. A furnished studio attic for sixty-five dollars a month, all utilities paid. Why had I left a high school teaching job in a beautiful little town nestled in the mountains along the Mississippi, in Minnesota? A town with a Danish bakery and a garage mechanic who knew my car. (He'd lift up the hood and check the car's insides when I parked on Main Street or in the church parking lot. Sometimes he'd leave a note under the windshield wiper.)

The "after college dream" simply wasn't Red Wing, Minnesota, I had decided by October of that first year. So I planned to leave, to find adventure, I told others. But I guess in my heart I knew I was looking for more than that.

I determined to run to glamorous, adventuresome places. I would study the world map. I pledged not to be a slave to my furniture, friends, family, or safe, small towns.

Maybe in far away places I would not be small-town Käären, the little-town school teacher. Käären, whose life seemed to be reduced to teaching five days and baking cookies for the sweet older ladies in her building on Saturdays.

Was this the "after college dream"?

Two of my closest friends had gotten married the summer we graduated from college. Two more times the bridesmaid. Later the pain in visiting them was in the leaving. For then, I was reminded I walked alone, I didn't have what they had. They were in the throes of fresh romance. I never had been.

If I'm going to be single, at least it will look *adventuresome and glamorous to them!* I continued to vow. And by early summer I packed one suitcase and convinced another single teacher to live, study, and travel Europe with me.

She lasted two months.

Sitting at the sea, my mind reconstructed the past and the haunt that never left me: aloneness.

Me. A withdrawn, insignificant, never-blooming high school student. The same in college. And then an insecure rookie teaching highschoolers when I was only a few years older than my students.

I kept believing there would be love and romance for me *after* college. So with this hope I could keep my insides from falling out all through high school and college, watching couples holding hands, magic and talk connecting their eyes, spirits, and souls. I could live through not belonging, not having a boyfriend whom my mother would love and brag about to her friends. Because I knew that after college, on my first job, it would be different.

I would be discovered. The time would be right. Someone would believe I was the most beautiful girl in the world. I would be cherished—someone's precious Christian wife.

Summer 1972

That first year of teaching I went through the motions, as they say. Directing plays, teaching kids to write greeting cards, and reading poetry in the city park to seniors in English 12.

Pleasant enough. But I could see the handwriting on the chalkboard. Me. The single. Never-married teacher. Spinster. Comfortable salary. Functional timepiece. Sensible shoes. Schoolteacher for fifty years. Retirement fund. Go to the Holy Land with the retired teachers tour group.

No matter how scared and young I was, I promised I would escape before I had more furniture, new car payments, and had arrived at the coveted job classification: MS Degree plus 50 on the pay scale.

Now France. Half a world away from anyone I knew, I was still singing the same songs. "Where is love?"

One day I left the sea and started to drag myself to class. As I had on so many Riviera days, I wandered into the little market shops so typical of France.

I spotted a beautiful French woman. *Lady! I mean, Madame,* I mentally confronted the woman. *You, yes you, my French lady smelling of rich perfume. You with the Pierre Cardin handbag! Are you alone too? But surely you must be loved. You look so loved. Who loves you? I'll bet he's a strong, handsome man who comes home and leaves his tie on for dinner. You're pretty. Are you loved because you're beautiful? Pretty girls marry well. That's a fact of life we learn at twelve. In America you would have been a homecoming queen. You would have had a boyfriend all through high school and been married when your skin was flawless and your face unlined. Madame, please don't notice me watching you. Let me study as you try on shoes and select a matching handbag.*

"Come to Paris with me! We'll transfer to the Sorbonne!" Ester, my classmate from England, encouraged, as I arrived late to class that day. "I'm going to leave tomorrow. We'll meet there! Okay?"

"Yes!" I jumped. Hope pumped through my body.

The train rocked, grinding and clanking through the night.

How impulsive I had been to join Ester in Paris. I rode with six other people in the "luxury" train sleeper. The sleeping compartment, which had shelves, not beds, had warnings in every language not to take off your clothes. So I slept with my coat wrapped around me and my purse for a pillow until what must have been 3:00 A.M. The sleeper compartment became hot and smelly. Two people were snoring. I wanted to scream, "Stop snoring, you oblivious idiots!" But they wouldn't have understood. A small Italian child whimpered. A French student coughed and hacked.

From the top bunk, I pushed open the sliding door and breathed the hall's smoky, stale air. It was better than the putrid air inside. The noise continued. Clanking iron against iron now combined with the noise of sleeping people.

At 6:00 A.M. the train pulled into the Gare de Lyon station. I hopped a cab to the student quarters and checked in. Five crooked wooden steps led me to my small room.

Three months passed. Old habits die cold, difficult deaths. I was still finding myself lost in thought on park benches and sidewalk cafés on the way to school.

One late fall morning, I didn't move off the edge of the bed. I was crying for my family. For Minnesota. For fellowship. Home. Hope.

"Dear God. I am alone. Help me. I know you are with me. I know you have a plan for my life. And it's not staring into space by the Seine or the Mediterranean Sea, singing sad songs," I prayed.

Paris is a long way from Worthington, Minnesota, where I grew up. In nearly two years of traveling I had grown introspective, withdrawn, and more lonely than ever.

"Oh, I go to the Louvre every Sunday. Paris is exciting and busy. My French is getting better. I go to the American Church in Paris on Sunday. I am having the time of my life!" I wrote on postcards to friends. Somehow writing such things made me feel better for short bursts. Little "highs," so fleeting.

But, after all, hadn't I also come to Europe to study French so I could possibly use it in foreign missions someday?

The two years passed with travel, trips, writing, and school. Dreaming. Moving from hope to fantasy and finally asking God, "Why? When? Would you make something special *for me?* Have you not given my friends beautiful little lives with purpose and direction? What are you going to do for me? When?

"I surrender, God," I continued. "I haven't moved you, even though I have been lost in lonely cities in far corners of the world coping with strange customs, language struggles, and black holes of paralyzing loneliness. God! You wouldn't be moved. You have stayed at the very center of my life. A constant. How far away must I go to convince you of what I need? Where is love, a home, a hearth for me?"

A front-page article in the *International Herald Tribune* caught my eye. Stranded students were being given half-fare flights on credit to return to the United States. Charter services had violated FCC regulations and left hundreds of students with no way home.

"I have a membership card for *this* organization!" I gasped when I read the list of those defaulting. Clawing inside my purse and wallet, I found the membership card.

"Oh, dear God! Is this my answer? Are you beginning to show me you do have a plan for my life?" I prayed aloud, squatting now with my purse contents spread on the hall floor. "Oh, no!" The membership card had expired two months ago!

"I'll take the Métro to the Pan American office! Maybe I still could qualify," I pleaded heavenward. "God, I do belong to you. Since I was a little girl I knew you, God. I sang songs to God and Jesus. But I'm a fledgling believer. A shaky little believer."

"Could I please return to America on one of your half-fare, one-credit tickets for stranded people?" I begged the airline agent in French, as I held the membership card with two hands hoping the agent wouldn't turn it over. "This organization was listed in the newspaper as one of the defaulting organizations responsible for stranding people, and I was going to go home with them—ah, possibly."

He took the card and turned it over. My heart sank. I still kept talking, but he wasn't listening. Then without looking up, he filled out a ticket! Paris to New York!

Dear God! Is this real? I thought. *Have I slipped completely from reality? People don't walk into an airline and get a ticket free—er, on credit—for half way around the world,* I prayed.

"Merci," I calmly whispered in spite of my inner hysteria. The ticket was mine.

Don't leave! Tell the agent you need a ticket to Minneapolis. How are you going to get from New York to Minneapolis otherwise? I commanded myself mentally before leaving the counter. *Speak! Get some guts! You have no choice, no money. Speak up!*

"Ah, er, Monsieur, s'il vous plaît," I stuttered, and explained how far New York was from Minneapolis, "my home," and how I was sure that he didn't fully have the distance perspective, living in a smaller country like France. A smile remained plastered across my face, so as not to enrage his French pride, by questioning his knowledge of geography.

"Mademoiselle! Si pas vrais! Oh, la la," he began yelling, thrashing his arms and stomping back to an office.

Two more French officials followed him back to the counter, all three talking simultaneously. (*So where are all those warm, moist French eyes, oozing with charm, now?* I wondered.)

All three officials continued to speak a once. I deciphered only a few words in the three minutes of nonstop, emotionally charged talking.

Suddenly the talking stopped. Two left. Another agent wrote a new ticket and handed it to me. He bid me "Bonjour," completely out of character with his previous, demonstrative display.

"Will I ever know the sweet hello that's meant for only me?" I laughingly sang on the plane. Good-bye Orly Airport. Good-bye Paris, my city that scared me, awed me. Paris—it's a long way from Worthington, Minnesota.

Home again. Minnesota—the tundra, but so what. Home is wonderful.

I began substitute teaching. I sent fifty dollars as partial payment to the Pan American office in New York.

"We have no record of your account, Miss Witte," the letter read. "We are returning your check."

"I was one of your passengers who returned home due to the charter problems," I explained on the phone. "Remember the plan? It was half-fare and on credit."

"Miss Witte, we will continue to investigate our records here in New York and through our Paris office. We will let you know when we find your records. If we don't find the records, well, just consider it 'on us'! " the office manager informed me.

I never heard from them again.

"Will I ever know the sweet hello that's meant for only me?"

Yes.

Spring 1973

Engagement

Within a few weeks of our first date, I got engaged to a fine young man from my church. I cried from that day until the engagement was broken a few weeks later.

"I just know there is a call on my life. I know Jesus has something else important for me to do with my life. It's not marriage right now," I sobbed, while agonizing with my fiancé and our pastor-counselor.

"Käaren, what are you going to do? You are an unemployed schoolteacher," my fiancé insisted. "Listen, you are going to marry me. I am going to take care of you. *That's* the plan for your life. I own a lovely new home and I have a promising career in medicine. You can put your life in my hands and be secure."

"But I think I'm supposed to be a writer," I continued, weeping and soaking Kleenexes.

"A writer? You've never published a thing!" he pressed.

"And furthermore I think I should work in radio and television," I asserted.

He retorted: "That's ridiculous. You're a simple, sweet, small-town girl, Käaren. What makes you think . . . Who said you could be in television and be a published writer?"

"Jesus," I whispered.

No one spoke. It was as if the mention of that name settled everything. Case closed.

The following year was spent in temporary office jobs—quite a challenge when I couldn't type and often couldn't even locate the remote office in the dark, frozen Minnesota mornings. The question *What or who makes you think you can write and be in television?* hammered in my head a thousand times. But then so did my answer: *Jesus.*

I had created a little television show on a local Minneapolis station after I went to France. It was a wonderful show involving old people and kids called "Years to Youth." The old people were spontaneous, warm, and still productive though in their eighties and nineties. The kids were cute and junior high school age. Although the show was canceled after that year, it had been my crack at television.

But now my future seemed relegated to temporary jobs in offices with gray metal desks and a stapler as a decorator item. I often thought this stage in my life was reminiscent of much of my early singleness. I never had one indication that the Lord was working. I was not "seeing." I was not "feeling" anything. But God was working. That simple, unshakable hope eclipsed any gnawing self-doubts.

"Do you have plans for lunch?" I smilingly asked one of the secretaries on the first day of another week-long temporary job.

"Yes, I do," she responded coldly, never looking up from her papers.

At noon the three other young secretaries gathered around her desk and discussed where they should eat.

"Let's go to Dayton's Salad Bar," one chirped. "Or we could go to the new little French café that just opened on the mall!"

Unanimously they agreed on the new café, grabbed their purses, and skipped out.

Have more pride! Bury your head in your papers. Don't let them think you want to go, I ordered myself.

But I didn't. I just watched them.

A friend, Martha, once pledged to me at summer camp when we were sixteen: "Always remember, Käaren, when your faith and hope weakens, I'll carry it for you. Käaren, I believe in great things for your life. You have all the earmarkings of a champion for Christ. Never forget this. I am your cup of hope in Christ's name." At that devastating moment in the secretarial pool, Martha's words found my soul. In fact, her words were to carry my heart many times in years to come.

Another year passed. My former fiancé questioned me: "Käaren, has the Lord shown you what you're supposed to do? What's the plan? As I told you two years ago, I'm not going to hang around and just be your boyfriend. I am now engaged to a beautiful girl. So, has your 'calling' been revealed?"

"No. There are no breakthroughs. I am still doing temporary jobs and occasional substitute teaching. And subbing is hard, because the kids draw naked pictures of me in the textbooks. What's so disturbing is they imagine me to be a lot chubbier than I am!" I joked, trying to lighten our conversation.

In the third year, he married.

That year I got a regular teaching job and began writing about my experiences in "the blackboard jungle." Magazines bought everything I could produce (after years of rejection slips!). I sent my school stories to Bethany House Publishers down the road from me in Minneapolis. Within a few months, *Angels in Faded Jeans* was released. Catapulted to the speaking circuit, I shared the platform with such people as Norman Vincent Peale, Zig Ziglar, and Catherine Marshall. The book became a best seller. Television appearances followed. I had to hire a secretary to help answer the piles of mail.

Years of speaking full-time and living life "on the road," sharing the promises of Jesus as I crisscrossed the nation and Canada, characterized my single life at this time.

"Käaren, your ship came in! I'll have to admit it." My former fiancé beamed as he placed his hand on my shoulder at a book autographing session. "Seriously, Käaren, I am proud of you. You waited with that little, naïve, blind faith of yours, like a four year old. I'm glad nobody could break you of it. Promise me you'll keep that faith of yours during the black hours, always."

"I promise," I choked, looking up from the table, my swimming eyes flowing into his.

God,
I trade my dreams and visions for yours.

— KH

Words Reveal Us

"I don't want Jesus Christ to return *now*," the young man I so longed to date insisted. "I want to get married first. And I pray to Jesus every day *not* to return until I get married!"

It's amazing. Our words tell on us. The mouth draws from what's in the heart, every time.

After the young man's statement I didn't pine to date him, for much was revealed in his little confession. Now I wouldn't need to date him to discover his values, heart, and relationship to Christ.

"What desperately shallow knowledge of Jesus Christ this man must have. He wants to postpone reigning with Jesus Christ and living in his glorious presence in exchange for a mere human relationship! How he has reduced the magnificent Jesus Christ! And what an unrealistic view of marriage," an objective counselor friend evaluated.

Must the pressure of singleness overshadow the return of Jesus?

Never.

Summer 1974

Amazing Grace

Korea. Short-term mission assignment.

It was a sunny, humid day. Twenty-five of us—journalists and Campus Crusade staff workers—and drove in a rickety, army surplus bus to visit a Korean orphanage. The mountains and the sun engulfed us. Our praise songs in six part harmony resonated, louder than the bus's engine.

Our high praise soared after a long, long rainy season. A special camaraderie bonded us, strangers but now family, sojourning in such a strange land of unwieldy language and customs. Somehow, in the bus ride we Americans, journalist-missionaries, became one.

At the orphanage, excited little children with big smiles circled the bus and pressed up to the door.

When we stepped off the bus, small hands reached for our shoulders, *felt* for our lapels, and pinned fresh flowers on us. They took our hands. Inside the doors, they used the walls to guide them. They were blind.

In a sparsely furnished room, we sat on crude wooden benches. Our "guides" joined those children in front of us. Angelic harmony flowed through hymn after hymn, in charmingly accented English.

Those little eyes, they never focused. Not one. In the front row one tiny child's eyes were permanently locked into an upward gaze. Their clothes didn't match. Their shoes didn't fit.

The last song went like this: "I once was lost, but now am found,/ Was blind, but now I see."

Back on the bus, nobody sang this time. Most wept all the way back to the city. We all felt it: amazing grace.

Spring 1977

Forgive Me, Jesus. Again.

Oh no! Not Lynn and Don! I gasped to myself, as I walked into the party.

I had once served on a church committee with Lynn. She was often uptight and demanded her rights frequently. We parted from the committee speaking to each other only when necessary.

The next year I served on another committee with Don. He did not make me feel important, needed, or worthwhile. I felt I could not work with another cutting, cold person, so I quietly resigned. In both cases, no words were exchanged, but each of us felt the other's lack of love.

When I first heard the news of their engagement, I thought sarcastically, *What a perfect match—two demanding, unsupportive people!*

When I arrived at the party, I scanned the room nervously for a chair. There was only one seat empty—right next to Lynn and Don. I awkwardly made my way to the vacant seat and exchanged cool greetings with the couple.

I was seated next to them only a few minutes when I began to feel the physical symptoms that the Holy Spirit's convicting power often brings to me. My face flushed and my pulse raced. My voice quivered. The coffee cup in my hand shook.

I should have sent them an engagement card. But then, they didn't send me a card or offer one word of sympathy when my mother died four weeks ago! I argued with myself inwardly. *But I should at least say, "Congratulations."* I remember when I was briefly engaged. The people who said nothing stand out in my mind to this day! I saw envy or jealousy on some of their faces. I certainly don't want to be in that class of people!

Lots of friends came up to congratulate Lynn and Don. The struggle continued between my thoughts and the Holy Spirit's reminder of my lasting bitterness, as people laughed and joked around me. *If I had had the slightest hint they would be here today, I would have stayed home. Anyway, I'm the one in mourning. If anybody should get attention, it should be me! Why do they sit there waiting for me to say "Congratulations"? They should express their sympathy to me before I express my congratulations to them. Wouldn't that be the Christian way? I'm sorrowing, and surely they don't expect me to turn my mourning into rejoicing.* I was rationalizing, and deep down I knew it.

People in the room chattered, their conversations rising and falling like waves, but I blocked it all out. My struggle continued, and the awkwardness of the situation became worse.

Lord, I don't want to change my attitude. I simply cannot choke out the word "congratulations." I nervously shifted position in my chair as the Holy Spirit's gentle persuasion pressed on my heart.

Okay, okay, I'll be the bigger person. I'll speak first, I grudgingly consented. With a strained smile, I gritted my teeth and forced myself to say, "Congratulations are due to both of you. What are your plans?"

"To get married," Don replied sarcastically.

The people nearby laughed. I was not amused at his reply, but I forced my smile to stay frozen in place. Silently I told the Lord, *I hope you saw the way he answered.* The party conversation shifted to other topics, and I sighed with relief. But the Holy Spirit let me know that my lesson in forgiveness wasn't finished yet. I had only spoken words. My heart's attitude was still riddled with bitterness. What should I do now?

The thought occurred to me that I had brought with me a

special engagement card for my dear friend Joyce, whom I had expected to be at the party. *Lord, you've got to be kidding! I can't give Lynn and Don that card. Besides, I signed it warmly and affectionately. I can't have Lynn and Don think I have any fondness for them after what they did to me. Besides, I'm sure I put Joyce's name on the envelope.*

The Lord spoke to me in his still, small voice: "If you don't forget the sins of others and let me bear them, then you add to my sorrows. Treat Lynn and Don as if it were I sitting next to you." I knew then how much I wanted to free myself from my bitterness.

"Jesus," I whispered. The uttering of that name lifted most of the petty irritations and bitter feelings I held in my heart toward Lynn and Don. "Jesus," I said again, quietly. Outwardly I continued to smile and look involved in a conversation going on in front of me. Inwardly my heart was broken. I felt forgiving tears well up in my eyes. *What will people think?* I fussed, as two tears slid down my face. My fingers wiped them away quickly. *Maybe people will think I'm still mourning for my mother.* But I knew these tears were different; they were releasing months of built-up resentment for the couple next to me.

I reached down in my purse for a Kleenex and saw the card I had brought for Joyce. To my surprise, I had not written Joyce's name anywhere on the card or the envelope. *Okay, Lord, I'll put that love and forgiveness into action! Lynn and Don will get this special card.*

I pulled it out of my purse and handed it to Lynn. "God bless you both," I said.

I didn't wait for her reply. I excused myself and went to help the hostess in the kitchen. While cutting the cake a few moments later, I felt two more tears of release roll down my face. "Jesus," I said again. "Thank you, Jesus."

Jesus,
   Thank you for believing in me. Thank you for counting on me.
       Amen

Once I know a promise of God, I can depend on it forever.

KH

Tough Times—Great Promises

Our sorrows and longings are felt greatest by God in God's heart.

My heroine, Hannah, in the Old Testament, so desperately wanted a child. Her husband could not understand it even though he loved her dearly. She continued to pour her heart into God's. She had to completely rely on him. (That's what an agonizing, longing heart makes us do.)

There are walls, no-escape routes, loved ones who can't comprehend.

The Christian life knows tough times.

A friend of mine illustrated how God's great heart answers tough times when she told me about her little boy, who had to wear excruciatingly painful leg braces. The child would scream in the night, and my friend would stand over his bed.

"Mom, you've got to take these braces off! I can't take the pain," he'd beg.

"Honey, I can't take them off, because I . . . I love you too much."

"Mom, I don't care about love. Please make the pain stop!"

"Honey, I can't take the braces off, because I have a dream—an exciting plan for your life," she comforted. "Honey, if I leave those braces on, you'll be able to run and become a strong, great man."

He screamed and moaned, "But Mommy, I don't care about any great dream! I just want to make the pain stop right now."

"Honey, I can't take the braces off, but what I promise to do is hold you and cry with you right through the night."

When people sacrifice their time for me, they give me part of their lives.

Winter 1978

Easy Rider and Me

"Hello, Marie. It's Saturday again. I'll be over soon," I said to my friend on the phone.

Driving on the freeway, I marveled at the sunshine. The temperature was barely above zero, but the sun was shining, and in Minnesota, in February, that is reason to rejoice.

But the next moment I was screaming, "Jesus, help me! Jesus, save me! Rescue me!" as I felt the car go out of control. Obviously, one of my tires had blown.

Still praying, I managed to bring the car to a safe stop. I hardly had time to breathe a shaky "Thank you, Lord," when I realized I was still in trouble. Big trouble.

My car had stalled at a spot just past a blind curve on the freeway, on a stretch which had no shoulder for emergency stops. Drivers were slamming on their brakes, horns were blowing and brakes screeching, as fast-moving cars came around the curve to find my stalled car in their way. They were moving too fast to stop, and the other lane was crowded at that time of day.

After nearly being hit twice, I jumped out of the car and ran around the curve to warn the drivers of oncoming cars. Finally, the driver of a van slowed down when he saw me and pulled in behind my car. I opened his door and quickly poured out my story. Only then did I take a good look at him.

Jesus, save me, I prayed silently. He was one of *them.* The dreaded. The feared. Black leather jacket, long beard, shoulder-length hair, dirty hands. Mean and scary. He was a member of the Hell's Angels.

"Get away from this curve," he hollered, "or you'll get killed."

The next moment a car nearly hit his van. He jumped out and roared: "Lady, you're going to get us both killed. Go direct traffic and throw me your keys. I'll change your tire."

It wasn't long before he was back. "I hate to break it to you, lady; the tire rim doesn't fit. You've got the wrong spare."

I ran to the car, while he took over directing the traffic. Suddenly, it was all too much for me: the flat tire, the cold, the danger, the ruined morning. I began to cry.

I know you'll get me out of this, Lord Jesus, but please hurry! I prayed.

I had recovered somewhat by the time the traffic slowed down a little, and my friend from the Hell's Angels ambled over. By this time, I had nicknamed him "Easy Rider."

"We'll just get a couple of drivers to phone for help," he said. But no one stopped.

Suddenly, I realized why God had allowed all this to happen.

"Sir, I want you to know why this happened. I've prayed every day for someone whom I could tell about Jesus Christ, my friend," I began.

"Oh, I get it. And today I'm 'it,' " he growled.

"Right! Today, you're 'it,' " I beamed, hoping to add a little levity.

I went on: "I used to be lost and lonely, looking for someone to love me. And then God's Spirit witnessed to me. He told me I could have a personal relationship with the Creator of the universe, a close, intimate association with a loving, caring Person who is free from hang-ups and who is always looking out for me. I could have a friendship with Jesus. What a friend! Right?" I was waving my arms at the sky, as the traffic continued to flow all around us.

"Jesus Christ promised that I could be a totally new

person. He promised he would never leave me. See? Even in a situation like this, he brought an 'angel' like you."

"A-a-a-h, lady, this is *Hell's* Angels," said Easy Rider, slapping his jacket. Despite his words, I seemed to detect a slight thawing.

"The Lord is a God of infinite variety," I said. "Sir, Christ is offering his friendship to you. It will meet your deepest personal needs. The ultimate test of friendship is the willingness of one friend to die for the other. Two thousand years ago Jesus Christ did just that for you and for me."

Easy Rider was still trying to get some of the drivers to stop. None of them did. They just took one look at this over-six-foot hulk of a man, who probably tipped the scales at 250 pounds, at his black leather Hell's Angel jacket, and quickly switched to the other lane.

Jesus, please make one of these cars stop, I prayed, as Easy Rider continued to direct traffic and curse the drivers.

"Not one lousy car will stop. Am I the only sucker in the world who will help you?" I knew why the cars wouldn't stop. He didn't.

I walked up behind him and tried to mouth the words, "I AM NOT WITH HIM," to oncoming drivers. They either didn't get what I was saying—or they didn't believe me.

I tapped Easy Rider's shoulder.

"I don't know how to say this, sir, but the drivers are afraid of you. Let's face it, you'd make Atilla the Hun look like an altar boy," I said, bracing myself for his response.

He laughed proudly. "I'm not used to being with so many 'straights.' Maybe you're right."

"If you hide behind the van," I suggested, "I know I'll get some cars to stop."

Sure enough, the next three cars stopped. I asked each driver to call for help. All we had to do now, while waiting, was to save his van, my Pinto, and our necks.

Easy Rider looked at me. "Tell me one thing, lady. Why did you have to get stalled on this particular curve?"

"Sir, that was because you were coming this way and would stop to help me."

"Oh, why do I ask?" he moaned.

I chuckled. "It's really nice of you to stay with me."

"You're darned right, it is," he said. "By the way, what kind of work do you do?"

"I write books," I said.

"Books? About what?"

"Experiences like this one. People like you."

"Man, why do I ask?"

I laughed. "Sir, don't you see? This story would hardly have been interesting if the leading character—you—had been your basic businessman in a three-piece suit. But look what you add to the story: terror, danger, intrigue, suspense, raw courage, and color. Lots of color."

By now, almost an hour had passed since the blow-out. I knew the ordeal was ending, that I could expect a tow truck to arrive very soon. The sun was still shining, we hadn't been killed, and I had gotten to talk about Jesus Christ to a member of the Hell's Angels. I felt wonderful.

"Sir, would it irritate you too much if I sang?" I asked. "Being in the great outdoors with this brilliant winter sun and being able to share Christ with you just makes me want to sing at the top of my lungs."

Easy Rider looked at me. "Listen, Good-News Susie," he said, "this isn't a Sunday school picnic."

"Oh, well, I just felt like singing praises. But if that will bug you—I won't."

"Oh, go ahead," said Easy Rider.

I lifted my head to the blue sky and belted out, *"Then sings my soul, my Savior God to Thee; How great Thou art, how great Thou art!"*

While my arms were still raised heavenward, a highway patrolman drove up and jumped out of his car.

"Officer," I began, putting an arm around Easy Rider's shoulder (I figured I was safe now), "you see a guy like this one, and immediately you think he's an animal, the Zodiac killer in a leather jacket. You picture guns, switchblades. But he's a real hero. He's been out here, helping me, for over an hour."

They both laughed as Easy Rider headed for his van. I dashed to my car, grabbed some money and a business card out of my purse. I opened the van door and handed Easy Rider the money. He refused to accept it or to give me his name.

"Don't be silly. I want to give you something," I said, leaving the money on the seat. "And here's my card. *When you find Jesus Christ, let me know. We're both waiting.*"

My next move shocked even me. Leaning across the seat in his van, I kissed him on the cheek. He smiled at me. And, for the first time, he looked me right in the eye.

"God loves you and so do I," I said, backing out.

He waved good-bye and flashed a big smile, showing two rows of even white teeth.

"Stick with him, Jesus. He's going to be one of us," I yelled as I watched the van take off down the road. I paid no attention to the patrolman standing beside me. I continued to yell, "See you in eternity, Easy Rider!"

And you know what? I believe I will. I really do.

Summer 1978

The Real Need

The beautiful, often-dated young woman or the handsome, socially skilled bachelor may live like many stars or celebrities.

After pieces of paper for autographs are passed to them through pressing crowds, they leave—alone. It may be lonely going home. They are not applauded or recognized by passing cars or by the gas station attendant or the check-out lady at Seven-Eleven.

They must return to the stage for another fix of recognition, because this says to them that they are loved.

But the high never lasts too long, for when the applause, the rush and crush of the crowds, and the cameras leave, they are alone again.

A whole lifetime may pass while the seeker of love searches for more audiences, more applause, or more relationships. New relationships. New heights of recognition.

The real need—that God-shaped, God-designed need—was never met. And that's the need *to love*.

Fall 1979

Let Him Find You

"Try this," I counseled Amy, a twenty-seven-year-old concerned about mating; "use the 'Let Him Find You' principle."

"It's the ultimate in trust. It calls for the spiritually courageous, the strong," I continued. "Walk. Operate. Live. Work. Socialize. Move. Talk. And most of all build the kingdom. Be relaxed—and you can be, because you are 'letting him find you.' "

"Are you the one?" I'd ask, charging over to complete strangers at the airport when I'd get off the plane for speaking engagements. "Are you the one who's come for me?"

"No," they'd inevitably answer, embarrassed.

I never selected the right one! I'd panic and push through the crowd hurriedly, looking for anyone who might possibly look like a host or a committee member.

Nowadays when I de-board a plane, I know, of course, someone's going to meet me. I relax and smile. I may even begin to stroll to the baggage claim.

Someone then always emerges from the crowd and says, "Hi! I'm here to meet you. I recognized you, Käaren!"

I may laugh a little while rejoicing that the old hysteria is history.

I let him find me. Now.

Winter 1980

Life, My Choice

Delores was fifty-one today. We celebrated her birthday at Becky's in Minneapolis—a restaurant dripping with elegance and antiques. The atmosphere was Delores's cup of tea. She's elegant. Good Italian leather shoes (Halston or Anne Klein, I'll bet) with purses to match. She has her blond hair done once a week. She's operatic, sings solos in a vibrant voice that people say is thrilling. She writes poetry and graduated with honors in English literature.

Delores has been in a mundane, uninteresting job at a large company for more than twenty years.

"Oh, I never wanted to advance in my job! I didn't want to pour my heart and soul into anything like a job, a ministry. I wanted to be open for marriage to some outstanding, successful man. I didn't want to be working overtime, getting exhausted, selling my soul. I wanted to be free to go a lot of places. You know, be at the right place and the right time to meet 'the Right One.' When I spotted that successful, great leader, I would be free to jump into his life and marriage!" Delores claimed when I questioned her lack of dreams and goals.

"But Delores, you could have done outstanding things with your music and writing," I protested. "Plus wouldn't some great achiever have been impressed with you? Wouldn't he want the qualities he built in his life, the discipline and the drive he demanded of himself, to be a part of his future wife?"

"Käaren, I only know that every year I thought, 'Why bother.' " She began avoiding the reference to being an outstanding woman. "This is the year I'm going to get married! This has *got* to be the year!"

The year never came.

What thoughts do I allow to enter my heart? A thought goes into an act. And action goes into character. And character determines destiny.

KH

Your Will Be Done

I fall into an emotional black hole sometimes.
Will I ever be loved by a great, fine, respected man?
Will I ever meet one in whose heart I will be at home?
There is a frenzy sometimes to find that home.
Now—this moment—I fear I can't find it.

God, in this darkness of my soul
I remind you of your promises.
My future depends on you,
    not a husband, children.
    (My "Isaacs.")
You are here with me.
Even when you don't make sense.
You promised you would not abandon me.
You promised you would care for me and hold my head up.

For I know all things work for the dream and plan God has for my life.
For I *know*.
I don't always "see."

Summer 1980

The Price

"Käaren, didn't you know *I* was dating Marty? Then *you* butted in. Don't you know that's not polite or Christian? And you're supposed to be an example around here. Ha! That's a joke," Emily raged, as she cornered me in the women's washroom in the church.

"I a-h-h-a-a," I stuttered. "Oh. Well, I a-a haven't ever even had a date with Marty. Never," I gasped. But she walked out in the middle of my sentence.

"Dear God, why does she hate me? God! Help me to see this situation correctly. There is more to this! I can't live with her hateful stares and stabbing words," I prayed, looking at myself in the washroom mirror before the evening service.

"Marty, why does Emily react so violently to me—especially when she sees me talking with you?" I questioned over coffee after church.

"I don't know, Käaren. I only went out with her a few times. I told her I didn't think we were right for each other." His features saddened.

"I just can't take these hateful stares and verbal lashings," I answered, my voice cracking with emotion. "There must be more to it. Her behavior is so exaggerated. She's acting out of proportion to the situation. Are you sure you two only went out casually a few times? There were no promises and no words of endearment?"

"Promises! Of course not. Just a few times we went out.

Very casual, no strings—that type of relationship," Marty insisted, shaking his head in confusion.

Two months passed.

"You've ruined Emily's life—her chance at love. You stole her boyfriend," one of her friends ranted in my face. "She and Marty were developing a beautiful, God-ordained relationship, then you moved in on Marty. I hope all the people in this church and all your readers of your phony books find out about the *real* you. And we're going to tell them."

My words came hard, slow and too late.

"Marty and I have never had a date," I whispered, praying my words would melt her hardness.

"That's a lie," she scoffed.

"Wait," I begged, as she stormed away leaving me alone in the dark church parking lot.

I watched her get in her station wagon and skid out of the lot.

Alone in the night, I cried to the sky and God: "Jesus, my Rescuer. I feel so helpless. Pour your Spirit into my being. I hurt. I hurt."

Earlier that day a staff minister called me into his office. Three of Emily's friends had "turned me in," reporting that I had broken up Emily's relationship with Marty.

"Käaren, this is serious," the minister stated. "These kinds of entanglements spread discord and strife among our people."

"Pastor, I never had an official date with Marty. They know that. Emily knows that. Sure, we stay together at single activities quite a bit, and occasionally we go out for coffee, but that's it! He's never mentioned dating and neither have I! I don't think we're right for each other anyway. Our backgrounds are entirely different and we're not going the same direction in life. Our personalities do blend, and we communicate well together and laugh a lot. I do admire his courage in changing his life-style. Before he became a born-again Christian four years ago, he lived deep

Summer 1980

in sin. He chose and committed to change those destructive, sinful patterns in his life," I countered.

"Well, I can't figure out then what caused Emily's frantic, almost hysterical anger," my pastor concluded, baffled. "Coldness and vacant eyes now characterize her."

"Pastor, this has been one of my most painful ordeals. Sure, I know what it feels like to die inside when the guy you like leaves you and patronizes another. Who in this culture's dating system has escaped that?" I moaned.

Another month passed. Hateful, icy stares replaced the reprimands of Emily's friends.

Emily, however, continued her venomous verbal abuse at Bible studies, picnics, and other activities.

"Other girls in this singles' ministry are wondering if you are going to break up their relationships with their boyfriends," she announced one day, sweeping her arm at the other people attending the singles' picnic.

A silence fell on everyone for about fifteen seconds. *Oh God, this is so humiliating, so unfair! God, answer my question! What has caused Emily to hate me far beyond what my actions deserve? What is so awful about me? It must be me,* I screamed in my head in those dead moments.

"Marty, I must ask you a confidential question," I began the next day. "Emily's reaction to you and to me is . . . so exaggerated. So hysterical. She still seems tenaciously attached to you. It's frightening, Marty." I gulped and hesitated.

"I know." He choked and tried covering it with a cough. "She hates me—but still wants me and wants to pursue a relationship."

Then he broke down emotionally.

"Oh, Käaren. You've figured it out, haven't you? Oh, Käaren. I couldn't tell you. I just couldn't," he sobbed, with his head in his hands.

"You and Emily had sex," I stated flatly, unquestioningly.

"Käaren, I had turned from that life of sexual sin four years ago. God delivered me. I was pure. And just one night I let myself fall into Satan's terrible trap. I did it. I chose it. I allowed that killing influence to enter my life again. I should have told you, but I couldn't. And look at the heartache this has caused. Käaren, sweet Käaren, forgive me. Jesus, please, please forgive me," he wailed and begged.

His crying, grieving confession lasted more than two hours.

While keeping this wrenching vigil, seeing this enormously strong, masculine man weeping, I thought: *Sex. It involves the very soul of a human, nothing less. A person's core. You can't cheat on sex. It gouges and shreds your inner fiber. A cutting and tearing through your soul is the price. And the result of immorality? Not satisfaction, but rather a deathly hurt and frustration. We never break God's laws. God's laws break us.*

Trust—It's Everything

"So, Käaren, what am I supposed to do—nothing? Just sit around and trust God to bring me my wonderful mate?" Alex, a twenty-four-four-year-old medical student raged at the suggestion.

"Alex! Trust is *not* to be belittled! Trust calls for the bravest, most courageous faith we can build into our characters. Nothing less. Don't call trust "nothing." It's everything," I confirmed to him, needing to remember it myself.

There's No Competition in the Family of God!

Singles' Sunday school class. We sipped morning coffee from styrofoam cups (a twentieth-century symbol of adulthood) and ate Winchell's doughnuts.

I sat next to Catherine, a thirty-year-old, single account-

ant who had logged ten years with me in the singles' group.
The Amen concluded our opening prayer.

We raised our heads. As we did, a tall, shapely young woman with flowing, waist length blond hair strolled down the aisle to the front row.

Catherine grabbed my hand. Her eyes burned into mine. After gaping again at the young woman (now with other pairs of eyes on her), Catherine bowed her head and prayed aloud, "Dear God, let her be stupid."

However You Choose to Reveal Yourself, God

I remember hiding behind other students in English class. I was afraid to give wrong answers and too shy when I knew the right ones.

The kids thought of me as withdrawn, shy, and bookish. Glasses. Plump. (Too much popcorn with Dr. Tom Dooley books and Rod McKuen poetry.)

By 1980 I had written my first book, done the national talk shows, and was out on the speaking circuit.

I was a late bloomer.

After one success rally, I was signing books at the platform. *What?! Is that him? No! It can't be!* I gasped mentally.

I was watching Ron Theissen moving down the aisle. The old shyness and insecurity, long buried, surfaced. I never said more than five words to this guy in high school. He was "Joe Cool." You know how cool he was? He was the guy in the late sixties with a bona fide muffler on his car. And he could use more than three words in a sentence. That qualified him as a "brain" in Worthington High School.

No, it just can't be, I continued questioning, as I stared.

"Käaren Witte! Shy, withdrawn, low-profile Käaren Witte! I can't believe this is you! I kept shaking my head and pounding it as I listened to you speak. I kept asking myself, 'Is this the same Käaren Witte from high school?' But I'll tell you, if this *is* you, then there is a God!" He laughingly exclaimed at my transformation.

We laughed together. He hugged me. The words from the song "If They Could See Me Now" played through my head. We talked about our lives; he told me he had become a Christian and was now happily married. We rejoiced.

As we parted, I recalled having a crush on him in high school. In fact, I determined to write a winning essay in English class so I could read it to the class while Ron sat in the front row.

"On Friday night I watched our star basketball player, Ron Theissen, making a beautiful swish shot. It didn't even touch the lace!" I exclaimed, as I blushed and my voice trembled . How I had changed from a tomboy to a femme fatale!

I laughed as I watched Ron exit through the huge auditorium doors. I smiled and said aloud to the empty auditorium, "You're right, Ron. There is a God. One who always keeps his promises. He plans and arranges unpredictable dreams for plump, ordinary, shy kids who needed to hide behind others."

My testimony will never be what I've "come out of," but who Christ is.

Home

While I was growing up, my Swedish grandmother, whom we called Mor-Mor, lived with us. When my mother was out of the house and Mor-Mor was answering the phone for her, she'd say, "No, Lilly ainta home!"

Mom said that when she was growing up in Chicago, the neighborhood kids would ride over on their bikes and yell from the alley, "Yoah—Li-i-il-le-e-e!" "Lilly ainta home!" Mor-Mor reportedly would call down from the kitchen window.

When one of us was looking for Mom, we'd ask, "Where's Mom?" and the other family members would jokingly answer in a Swedish accent, "Lilly ainta home!"

On October 1, 1977, we said good-bye to our mom. She died in our arms, the whole family's arms—as a believer following Jesus Christ to the end.

Mor-Mor had "gone home" some fifteen years earlier.

I cried every day for two years after Mom died. But I know that on that October day, dear Mor-Mor finally said, "Lilly. She's home."

Me

Me.
I struggle.
I fail.
I doubt.
I need, long.
No sinless past.
Not squeaky clean.
No halo.
No name up in lights, spiritually speaking.
But I read about the sinners whom Jesus forgave
    simply because they believed.
I'm just basic and common enough to believe.

Spring 1981

Please, God, a Friend for Mom and Dad

"Dad, do something with him! Mom can't face people in church or the grocery store. I have the highest absentee record in school," I sobbed to my dad regarding my brother, who was in trouble not only at school but also with the law.

"Mom, do something! Send him away," I begged.

"Oh, honey, I wish I had some comforting friends. I wish you wouldn't also keep saying, 'Do something!' I have prayed and prayed. We have done our best as parents. We've got to believe in the promises of God," Mom would say, weeping. "Honey, I've cried out to God for people from this town and church. How I needed their confirmation and support. How I needed to hear somebody say, "You and Al are good people—and your boy is going to turn out fine." I guess people don't know what to say. Or maybe we haven't been good parents. I just don't know at this point. I just don't know."

She seemed so frail and vulnerable then. Mom had always been emotionally sturdy, positive and giving. Grandly dressed, she was a gracious hostess, moving with ease in her elegantly furnished home. She laughed easily and was an athlete: biking, skating, swimming. I thought as I watched her shaking and weeping, *She once looked immortal; now, so vulnerable.*

The majority of the people in our little church were young in those days. Their kids were babies, cuddly and pink. Cute tots in velvet dresses and tiny patent leather shoes. What did they know? In those days.

"No wonder the people didn't talk to us much. They didn't know what I was going through as the mother of a teen," Mom continued. "I didn't tell your dad this, but one of the ladies took me aside and said, 'You should have been stricter with your boy, Lilly. Then you and Al wouldn't have failed as parents.' "

I remember when one of the town's doctors gave me a ride home from youth group.

"Wait, I'll get your record album! It got mixed with my stack at the youth party Friday night," I called back as I was running into our house.

The doctor's station wagon was loaded with his three small children and three other church teens. I handed him the record, after digging through the albums and scrambling back to the car. Panting and smiling, I stood at the car window as he opened the record jacket.

"What? There are *two records* in here! You put *two* records in *one* album cover," he exploded.

"No, I didn't—" I started to say, feeling crushed.

"Well, it sure looks like you did," he interrupted, raging. "What a stupid thing to do. Don't they teach you responsibility and respect for others in that family of yours? You're going to be like your brother: a nothing, a mess."

"But I didn't put two records in there; it must have been someone at the party," I pleaded, as six pairs of eyes burned into my face.

"Now she tries to lie her way out of it," he announced, turning around and addressing the other kids.

"I'm sor-r-r-y," I stuttered, feeling stunned and humiliated. He didn't answer. He just kept looking backward as he drove out of the driveway.

So often in those days of despair I would question, "Why God? Why does this happen to me?"

I graduated from high school and college in that town, then our family moved and I never returned until 1981, many years later.

"This is Mrs. Stone. Do you remember me?" a sweet and

hauntingly familiar voice asked me over the phone one day.
"What a surprise!" I answered.
"I'm chairman of the banquet committee. We have followed you and read your wonderful books. We want to have you as our keynote speaker this year," she cheered.

I want to return to my hometown! I have much to share. I mentally rejoiced. *I know what my message is already!*

How old the people have grown, I thought, staggered at seeing them again. *They probably were my age when I left.*

We hugged. Sometimes they had to remind me of their names. Soft tears slipped out the sides of my eyes.

"We didn't know what your family was experiencing years ago, Käaren," Elsie said as she wept, holding me in her arms in the church kitchen before I was to speak.

Brokenly, she added, "Since your family lived here we had . . . Two of our children experienced divorce. One is on her third marriage. Another daughter is on drugs. Oh, Käaren, *all* of our children were small fifteen years ago, so we just blamed your parents for your brother's adolescent behavior. My story is not the only one. So many of the church's families are living with rebellious, wayward children. Their hearts are breaking. Please forgive us. We just didn't know."

Fifteen years later I testified to broken, defeated hearts: "He is a God who can be trusted. You have been good, Christian parents. God will bring your children home. Today my brother is a Christian. No, my mother didn't live to see it, but then again, I'm going to believe she does see it."

Tough Times

Tell me about your Christian life. Does it have tough times, sorrow, and distress?

If so, I'll believe God has a great purpose in your life.

People who strive to avoid problems seldom find the "God of Enough"—*El Shaddai.*

Hard times are our opportunity to see what we're made of.

"God never uses people greatly until they hurt deeply," a great Christian once said.

Do I want to affect the world in some pure, genuine, authentic way?

Yes.

Hurt-filled seasons cause me to love more deeply and purely. They put me in touch with my every human emotion.

Thank you, Mom and Dad, for never making digs, jokes, or cuts about each other in front of us kids or in public. I never saw cracks in your foundation.

Summer 1981

The Royal Wedding

Diana and Prince Charles got married today. A royal wedding—the world watched. So did I.

"Käaren, this is DeAnn," my friend from as far back as sixth grade announced on the phone. "Are you watching the royal wedding?"

"I am," I lamented.

"I called . . . Well, I knew you'd be watching. Tell me . . . ah, how do you feel?" Dee inquired.

"Oh Dee, can you imagine a royal wedding? The royal coach! The gowns! Diana's gown! The royal family! The pageantry! The world watching! Oh, Dee. To be royalty . . ." I cried. (But I pumped my tears to the back of my throat.)

"But Käaren. Dear Käaren. My friend. You have been born into royal blood, at a great cost," Dee whispered.

My Greatest Answer to Prayer (So Far)

"I'm sorry you lost your mother," a woman at the graveside said after we exchanged explanations as to why each of us was there. "I lost my little girl when she was only four. I'm sorry you lost your mother."

"I didn't lose her. I know where she is," I whispered.

I held the woman's hand in mine, excused myself, and walked down the cemetery road on what would be the last warm day before the Minnesota snows. It would be the last time I would stand by my mother's grave and not scoop off the snow to view the bronze plaque that read "Lilly Witte. Born Again." I sang the words, "When I fly to worlds unknown and behold him at Thy throne."

Few moments in my life have been as indelible and emotional as that one with the nameless woman. My mind couldn't comprehend what was happening. The words "I know where she is" were a lullaby.

I kept praying. "God! Jesus! I know where Mom is, but there is dear Dad here on earth. Jesus, hear me! He's alone. Tell me, who is listening to him? Who is caring for him, making him feel special, admired, and important? What kind of food is he eating? Is there anyone to make him pot roast suppers and fresh peach pies? I can't bear to go to his house! I'm afraid I will find him crying in the garage or the basement. I can't bear to hear my dear dad grieving."

Opening the Bible to my settling date, I would pray again with the promise, "God is blessing above and beyond what I could dream or hope for"—for my Dad, for me, for our little family (Ephesians 3:20 TLB). "Dear God, lead him to a wonderful new mate, a precious Christian lady who loves you."

"Thank you ahead of time, great God, for the answer." I continued to soar. "I know you are arranging for him. I am going to praise you for the answer right now. I am expecting! I am 'seeing' and proclaiming the answer as you instructed us to do in Mark 11:23!"

Three years passed with the praises, and, yes, the prayers were peppered with cries and bouts of fear. But they were quieted with promises and praise, every time.

"Honey, when I was on business in Tulsa, friends introduced me to a wonderful lady. She's so sunny and sweet. A lovely Christian!" my dad announced on the phone.

"Dad, that's great. Does she have any daughters?" I pressed, stifling some giggles.

"Ha!" He chuckled, recalling an old memory. "Yes! She does. She has two daughters and a son."

"She's perfect," I marveled, delighted at the prospect of having sisters in my life (I had pleaded with my mother for a sister until she was fifty-one).

"We're praying and seeking the Lord's direction in our relationship. I know you'll pray for us, too," Dad continued.

Four years after my mother's death, God had performed my miracle. My dad was remarried. I quickly called the publisher just as my second book, *Great Leaps in a Single Bound*, was to be released.

"I know it's too late to add anything to the book, but maybe you could add something at the bottom of the dedication page!" I pushed and cajoled alternately.

"I think we could arrange that," my editor agreed.

"Here it is! It's Psalm 40 fulfilled: 'Tell everyone the good things the Lord has arranged!' The last dedication item will be 'To Mrs. Hazel Witte: The greatest answer to prayer in my life so far. She would have been my mom's best friend—I just know it. They're both angels. I'll call her MOM II!' " I rejoiced.

The problem with rejoicing on the phone is you can't jump up and down and raise two hands or applaud in praise.

The only thing we take out of this life is relationships.

Christmas 1981

Wistful Rejoicing

"Dad, you sound great—on top, very happy," I remarked, chatting with my dad on the phone.

"Last night we went to a party," he continued. "You should have seen Hazel! She looked gorgeous. God blessed me! I mean, I walk in with her and I know everybody's thinking, 'What a doll!' What a knock-out she is!"

"Dad, that's beautiful." I laughed, then soberly said, "I hope somebody says that about me some day."

He said somebody would.

The Me Nobody Knows

Some moments
I am sure the loneliest place
in the whole world
is this human heart of mine.
This frigid Minnesota day triggers wondering.
   Wonderings . . . Ah, but they've come plenty on July days too . . .
"God, do you have a special man planned for me? A home we will build together with bookshelves, framed watercolors, and a couch with big matching pillows? Easy-listening music and laughter from a joke we heard that day? A kitchen decorated in red and calico? Wooden spoons in ceramic pots? And eyes and arms to meet mine?"
At these moments, I just exist.
No sparkle, no glow. A low-grade fever of blandness.
I don't feel. I just fill up space.
No one has condemned me, saying, "Christians shouldn't feel that way, Käaren."
I wrestle with self-pity. I know it lies to me and exaggerates.
   I realize sorrow and aloneness are part of every human being.
   The song came on the radio. At this moment. The singer sang, "You're the best thing that ever happened to me."
   "Jesus, will anyone in your universe ever say that to me? Will one?" Then I heard Jesus say to me, "Käaren, you're the best thing that ever happened to *me*."

I heard him.
My sadness lifted.
And the tears I found on my face—I didn't remember
    how or why they got there.
Rainbows always follow my rain
    and I forget I even got wet.

Good-Bye, Five-Buckle Overshoes; Hello, Cowboy Boots

(Farewell letter to my singles' group in Minneapolis, Minnesota.) "Is God going to do anything with me? If I'm going to remain single, doesn't he have some special plan for my life? Is anything going to happen to me? What is God doing with me? It looks like a big nothing." I cried in huge gasps on my bed ten years ago, while my friend Jan Markell sat and listened.

"Käaren, take God at his word. Believe him—will you? He'll keep his promises to you," Jan persuaded.

A few weeks later the Lord literally dropped some television programming ideas into my head *after* I called WCCO–TV and told them I had "fresh ideas for new programming." After a year working at WCCO I was back to teaching. And back to crying.

"Käaren, listen, I believe in you, and Jesus believes in you," Jan counseled again. "And he only operates in one style in the lives of his children. And Käaren, I'm telling you what you told me a few years ago when I was a struggling, unpublished writer of free verse. Käaren, you've got to keep trusting God. He does have great surprises in store for your life, no matter how it looks now."

So while teaching junior high, I found my little ministry and mission field to be my classroom.

Then my world stopped. My young, athletic mother died.

"What's a house without a mother? She's the heartbeat and sunshine of the house. We'll never have anything but crying, sorrow, and sadness," I sobbed to my dear dad, as the rest of the funeral party left, and we stood alone at the graveside.

But God planned to heal us—in his inimitable style.

During those three years of healing, my life went by without any indication that God had something special in mind. *(And why should he? Who am I? A small-town kid who never made all* A's *and never was a cheerleader,* I'd doubt in dark moments.)

I chose to leave the darkness. I walked in faith and trust with my hand in his and my eyes closed. I shared this faith with the little blackboard-jungle kids in my junior high. Then I got a pink slip. My school was closing due to enrollment decline. The faculty asked, "What are you going to do?"

"I'm a believer in Jesus Christ. His very Spirit is operating in my life. He has a perfect track record, too, in my life. He's got something planned," I answered. But I thought, *Vo-tech, here I come.*

That spring I sent my blackboard-jungle stories to a book publisher. The timing was right! Within a few months my first book, *Angels in Faded Jeans,* was released. I then began crisscrossing the country speaking and appearing on television and radio programs. The timing was right!

Because I was single, I was often asked to speak to singles. So I wrote another manuscript called *Life in the Single Lane* and sent it to a publisher. However, one day while sitting in my kitchen the title *Great Leaps in a Single Bound* was dropped into my head.

"Now *that's* the title of my singles' book! That's what I want to say to my readers!" I argued to my roommate.

I contacted the publisher. "Send back that 'single lane' manuscript," I insisted.

"But we like it!" they insisted.

"But it's not my *real* heart, my insides," I pleaded.

Within a few months I sent *Great Leaps in a Single Bound* to the publisher, and in April 1982 it was released. The timing was right!

But I was panicky. When you write, you write in private. After publication you think, "Oh, no, what have I said?"

Besides my new book in April, I got an invitation from *Solo* magazine, a Christian magazine for singles, to consider the position of editor.

"No way," I thought. "I want to move to L.A. Sunny Cal, kids. Plus I want to do more television, Lord willing. And furthermore I don't need a job."

A few days later my pastor friend, Bob Crumbley, called: "Käaren, this is an opportunity for you! Can't you see it?"

"You're right," I concluded after his counseling.

I didn't even know where *Solo* was located, but I found out and flew down for an interview.

The publisher of *Solo* knew. The staff knew. And I knew. It was a match, *Solo* and I. (And you guessed it—the timing was right.)

I would have taken this position in any city in the world! But do you know where the headquarters of *Solo* are?

Tulsa!

It's a miracle. (But what do we expect when we put our lives in the hands of this incredible Christ, who always keeps his promises—somehow, sometime, someplace, someway, but always.)

Dear friends, I want you to know something. I know what it is to struggle with God, trying to manipulate him and give him clues, tips, and game plans for your life. I know what it is to be a single in a coupled world. I know what it is to be awakened in the night by sounds, only to find it is your own sobbing.

But I have learned—on these ordinary days that run into ordinary Friday nights that run into uneventful Saturday nights and weeks and years—that God is behind the scenes working and pulling for us. He is arranging, connecting, planning, dreaming, and preparing. Never doubt that (Ephesians 3:20 promises). Live with an air of expectancy. With radiant praise, open yourself up to miracles and dreams.

So dear friends, don't consider this a good-bye. This is really an invitation to believe with me for those great happenings in all of our lives.

In addition to this invitation, let this letter also be a thank you. Thank you for being my friends and cheering me on in my great leaps in a single bound.

And after all is said and done, please remember me for one thing: loving you.

Love always, I promise,
Käaren

Questions?

Spring 1982

Boxes

Tulsa, Oklahoma. New job: Magazine editor. New city. New apartment.

"That's where I want to live—in that round high-rise overlooking downtown Tulsa and the Arkansas River," I exclaimed to my folks as we drove around the *Solo* magazine office area.

I moved in, twenty-three floors up. I unpacked my boxes and called the apartment lobby office. "You can take the empty boxes now. Thank you."

There was a knock on the door. "We've come for the boxes," a heroic male voice reported.

"No, I'm not ready," I gasped, opening the door with all the empty boxes stacked behind me.

"We can take what you have ready. It looks like there are quite a few empty," he exclaimed, viewing about forty boxes stacked to the ceiling.

"Oh. No . . . ah . . . I'm not ready . . . ah, not the kind of ready you're thinking of . . . I mean, not ready emotionally!" I stuttered, trying to identify my feelings.

"What do emotions have to do with boxes, lady?" he snickered, questioning eyes rolling to the four corners.

"I'm sorry to bring you up here. But please, ah . . . I'll call you when I'm really ready." I ended the conversation by closing the door while I was mid-sentence.

Giving up my boxes . . . good, sturdy boxes. Many wax coated. Some from professional movers at four bucks each.

It's so final, parting with one's boxes. Many I had stored in my attic in my Minneapolis house.

Lord, I suppose I'm not trusting you. That's what it means, if I can't give up my boxes, right? For if I have boxes I can move easily. I won't feel so forever stuck in an apartment alone. That's why I can't give them up. I am making a statement about the rest of my life: I'll be in an apartment. Alone. With floors and floors of widows and old-vintage women.

Wait! Maybe I can get them into my one empty storage closet! I jumped. (Exactly six boxes out of forty fit.)

Face it, Käaren. Face it. The Lord is trying to tell you something. When are you going to be a perfect little soldier? No questions. So what if you spend the next forty years in this building? Then you can retire here. It even has wheelchair ramps. And the apartment building van takes the retired ladies and gents shopping every Wednesday noon for their groceries and then to lunch at Furr's Cafeteria, and at Christmas the van takes them on a tour to see the Christmas lights of Tulsa. Get the picture? Accept it and be content, I commanded myself.

Lord God, did you give me this beautiful apartment, with the view and pool and bike paths, just to hide truth? A slick way of getting me to move in here without my having a sneaking suspicion this is my future. Pacemaker paradise. And I've got forty years to grow into it.

And now they've come for my boxes. Boxes that represented quick moves. Moves full of hope, promise, and adventure. I always felt mentally I could move anywhere in a few weeks—because after all I already had my boxes!

But not now.

Oh. *But whoever heard of folding boxes? These boxes can't fold,* I responded inwardly to the still small voice.

Fold the boxes, the still, small voice suggested in my mind.

But sturdy moving boxes just don't fold. Flimsy department store boxes fold, not these, I insisted.

Fold the boxes—over and over in my mind—*Fold the boxes.*

After scrambling for a serrated-edge freezer knife, I slashed the first box bottom, then pushed it flat. A perfect flat box! It needed only some sturdy tape to be ready at a moment's notice.

Forty sturdy boxes now rest beneath my bed. Folded.

(You have to be single a while to fully understand this one: The emotional attachment to boxes.)

Summer 1982

Dating

"Gene, I try not to date indiscriminately," I began.

"What! You *try not* to date?" Gene cross-examined me. "How are you going to meet someone? You do want to get married, don't you? I can't believe this. I've never heard of such a program."

"Let me explain, Gene," I pleaded. "I know it's contrary to anything you've heard. Five years ago I felt the Lord impressing on me to date carefully, to invest my time wisely, to watch my emotions. I had so often tried to date certain men. Tried to be what I speculated they wanted. I tried to be in the right place at the right time. Spare no expense. Money for new clothes—no problem. Travel, motels, plane fares, rental cars . . . I tried. Nothing worked. Men would feel hunted and run.

"Sometimes the man would be interested in our relationship," I continued, "and then I'd back out. What was left? Hurt feelings. Guilt."

So often I see how dating is the world's game. The world knows nothing of the supernatural leading of Jesus Christ. Think about dating. When two people go out, they either accept or reject each other. I don't want to reject any one. I don't want to be rejected. The dating system forces fragile human egos to be placed on auction blocks.

I believe Christ has a supernatural plan for bringing people together. He does for everything else.

He is not only able. He is *willing*.

CBA

"I'll meet you in Dallas on Sunday night. I'll take you out to dinner," a Christian businessman said to me.

"Great, that will be fun."

"What hotel are you staying at?" he asked as he left the *Solo* offices.

"The Plaza."

"Great. I'll be staying there, too. See you Sunday night."

I went to Dallas early for that convention. I spoke to singles Friday and Saturday night. I was agonizing. As Sunday night drew to a close, I knew I had made the wrong decision.

You know you are attracted to this guy, Käaren Witte. He is married. He is fun and warm. He likes you. And you like him.

Sunday I spoke. What did I speak about? "Don't put yourself in positions where your human nature can take over. Check your foundation for cracks."

"How do you handle your emotions?" the businessman had asked me on one occasion at lunch.

"What do you mean?" I asked, but mentally I thought, *He's referring to sex—don't be so naïve, Käaren. He's a new Christian. As a single, he didn't follow Christian standards.*

Sunday passed. I was struggling. *But God! I'm alone in this city. Am I supposed to go down yet another time to the hotel dining room? When he calls, how will I say, "I'd better not"?*

Sunday afternoon I waited in the hotel room for his call. The call never came. I went to the dining room and cried when the waitress finished taking my order. I ordered a salad and speculated that the people around me thought I was perhaps "hotel property." I mean, how many women with long hair and wearing a sundress do you see eating alone in the hotel dining room? I finished and walked to the elevator. Alone in the elevator, I let the huge sobs come. "Dear God, I would rather be the loneliest person in the world. I would rather feel a hundred times worse than I feel right now than feel guilt knowing that I was making cracks in my foundation and harming anything so fragile as my delicate human psyche."

When I returned to Tulsa, he called. By then the feelings and the plan—recognizing the cracks—were evident to me. "People said they saw you at the convention. I left messages for you at the Plaza. You weren't there."

Yes, I stayed at the Plaza, but I learned something when I got back to Tulsa. There were two Plazas.

Examine everything for the fingerprints of the enemy.

I don't want to create an image. I want to create character.

— KH

Travel

When I'm running late at an airport, I'm assigned to a gate they haven't finished building yet. When I'm early, it's gate one.

When I'm late I run the mile in 8.9 with three pieces of carry-on luggage, a bag of oranges, hot rollers, and a two-pound library book!

At the hotel I search out the window. Where am I? Trips now bring me only passing friendships and people who need to tell their life stories to me in three minutes or less.

People think I'm something special now because of the media attention I have received. I'm scared they'll find out I'm a nobody. I grieve when they are nervous, uncomfortable, and intimidated around me. Why do they have to choose language that's lofty when addressing me? Why do they search for ways to speak that make them sound like Harvard scholars?

Sometimes between meetings I go to the hotel pool. The other business people swim and make plans to join one another for dinner.

I go back to my hotel room. (They asked in the pool what I did. I told them Christian books and ministry.) I look for a scrap of anything in the bottom of my purse. Just maybe some half-ounce package of honey-coated peanuts from the last flight. Maybe a Lifesaver will kill my hunger. Maybe sleep will come quickly.

I don't find hotels glamorous. I find them lonely places. Places where I must make choices.

Longings

Today I read Luci Swindoll's new book, *Wide My World, Narrow My Bed*. I met Luci yesterday. She was bubbly, lovely. Her warmth and beautiful Scandinavian appearance drew people to her.

We chatted. We giggled about the calories in the melting ice-cream cones that were running down our hands in the Dallas heat.

I read the book in one sitting. I couldn't put it down, and I had one question that I needed answered. Luci articulated a rich, full Christian single life of travel, friends, humor, career, and family. I finished the last chapter. I loved Luci. But my question never got answered: "Doesn't she ever long—and pray—for a wonderful Christian husband?"

No longings. I wonder—what must that be like?

As Far as You Can See

We're impatient. We're quick to change jobs, homes, friends, churches. But God will not and cannot be the sovereign God if he conforms to our petty plans. He is sovereign. He rules—even when *my* dreams become dusty with discouragement.

God promised Abraham in the Old Testament, "Abraham, the land is yours as far as you can see."

He says the same thing to us today. "The land," our divinely inspired dream, is ours as far as we can "see" and dream.

"Seeing"—this is the stuff dreams are made of.

Compromise (Looking Back)

So many things are important, desperately important, when a prospective young man likes me. My size and clothes must be perfect. I must have new clothes ("Oh God, lead me to new clothes")—smart, expensive outfits. And my folks—they must be perfect. Exquisite in schooling, manners, and dress. There must be fabulous conversation, witticisms, pleasantries. All the appropriate smiles and graces. And my house—Oh, dear God, don't let him think we are not fabulously wealthy. Don't let anybody blab about huge financial losses a few years ago. And nobody mention that sometimes I get to be fifteen to twenty pounds overweight and have three sizes of clothes in my closet and even two sizes of underwear. Ever. And he must think I never sweat. If I sweat at all, I smell like violets—even playing tennis. My sweat glands produce fragrances. There is no bacteria EVER on my skin to make any smells.

"Do I like football? What a question. I love to spend Saturday, Sunday, and Monday nights watching football. Why, of course I'm mad for the games. The Minnesota Twins has always been my favorite football team."

Why were dating and mating so desperately important?

I hated it. I was nervous and frayed on dates. Trying. Trying so desperately to be what I guessed—after careful calculation and observation—that this guy would want in a girlfriend and a wife. I did this into my twenties. Striving. Planning. Plotting.

"I am not rich, Käaren," a guy would say.

"Oh. Goodness, I'm poor too."

Or, "I've worked hard, Käaren. I have made money. God has blessed my business. I am afraid sometimes women date me because I'm rich," another would confess.

"Oh. Goodness, I'm doing well myself. The Lord has blessed me. I don't need to date your for your money!"

Or, "My dream wife is a simple, quiet Southern-belle type who bakes cupcakes and makes soup from chicken necks. I don't want one of these high falutin' females who wants to set the world on fire with some high-powered career."

"Well, sakes alive. Lil' ol' me. I've got some mighty fine cupcake recipes, tried and true, tested by dear Daddy himself from the fine ovens of Mommy homemaker herself!"

Or, "I love to wear grubs—jeans and tee-shirts. I hate dressing up. I even wear grubs to church if I feel like it! I refuse not to be myself."

And I'd lie to another guy.

That was five or more years ago. Today I will say it. I have dreams—big dreams. I not only want to bake cupcakes and make homemade soup, but I want to speak at the White House! (Well, why not the White House? Would you put anything past the Lord? Neither would I.)

You know what? I hate football. And if you wear only jeans and grubs, fine. Do so. But that's not "me." I can now say it!

"What if everyone's in grubs at this gathering, Käaren?" someone once asked.

"Unless we're washing the car or gardening, I refuse to wear those kinds of clothes," I responded.

"But, Käaren, *everybody's* wearing them!" she continued. "You'll be dressed wrong. You'll be odd, out of it!"

"I don't see it that way! I'll be dressed right, and they'll all be wrong! Let them come up to my standards," I insisted.

For years I compromised. I would be what men wanted me to be. I was so afraid to tell them about my dreams—these ideas with which God and I soar. I was afraid to tell them about the White House. So I compromised. I was afraid and insecure to become all God dreamed for me. The risk and possible cost: a husband, a home. But compromise is sin.

Today what I want is to become all God dreams for me. To risk!

Someday, somebody will dream with me. We'll be dreamers together. Unashamed. Uninhibited. Unguarded. Risking wildly! Because we will know these dreams are God's.

And we'll say we didn't compromise.

I bump into happiness when I ask someone, "What's one nice thing I could do for you today?"

When I sacrifice my time for another, I forget about myself and wave hello to joy.

Fall 1982

Watching Over

When I was six years old, I woke up late one night. A light glowed down the hall in Mom and Dad's bedroom.

There were no sounds.

I slipped out of bed and peeked in their door. My dad sat next to the bed.

"Daddy, what's wrong with Mom?" I questioned.

"Nothing, honey," he whispered.

"Then why are you staring at Mom?" I probed.

"I just like to watch her sleep sometimes, that's all, sweetheart." He smiled sheepishly.

"OK." I smiled back. Satisfied, I snuggled into bed again.

In all my years to come, I prayed for the kind of husband who would "just watch" in the night.

Mother, I Never Knew You

Five years have passed since my mother died. A part of me died then, too.

I could say what I've said before. "She was too young. I was still single. She wasn't healed . . . and how we prayed . . ." But these thoughts have all been thrashed through, struggled with, then settled.

It's a sunny fall afternoon today in my new city, Tulsa. Warm sun does it. It takes me on the backroads of my memories. So I flipped through photo albums and studied the pictures of my family. I opened a drawer I use daily, but today I reached further down. I wanted to move my heart into the past. I wanted to remember something about my life when I was eleven, then thirteen and fifteen. Some event. Some hope. Some imagined boyfriend. Looking at some pictures make me laugh out loud. But all say something about time. And life.

I held up a picture. I'm ten years old. My mother is standing with my dad in front of the White House. They're midwesterners. Tourists.

Look in her face, I instructed myself. *Who was she? What were her hopes, dreams, fears, doubts, visions, goals, hurts, and longings? What were her secret roads? Who did she love in her childhood? Who held her? Who kissed her and made her believe she was a beautiful little girl? What did she dream for my dad? For me? For my brother? What was she feeling when Auntie Florence died, and Grandma, and Uncle Chester? Did she want to be First Lady, married to the president of the United States? Did she want to be an Ambassador to Sweden? Did she want to climb Mount Rainier? Did she want to be an anthropologist studying the rain forests of the Philippines?*

Why didn't I ask her any deep, soul-on-soul questions? Was it because maybe, just maybe, I would hit a raw nerve and we'd both cry?

Our emotions were close to the surface in those youthful days. My little family had experienced, I suppose, what most human beings encounter sometime in their lives: hurts, the loss of loved ones, defeats, a rebellious youngster, financial losses, the crying out to God—judging him and his faithfulness before one sees the total picture. Before one gives him time. We doubted in the dark.

I looked at another picture. "Mommy, you're beautiful," I said out loud. "Your hair is rich and bouncing. Such elegant posture. Enormous eyes. Flashing smile." Her presence—just her walking by in a room made me feel content.

Mommy. Refusing to be complicated. Mommy. Holding all of our heads up, lifting our spirits. Her faith eclipsing doubt. Mother—how the emotional needs of her children drew them to her.

I remember our soft moments. She'd sit on my bed before I slept. We'd talk about quilts we'd make, my home "when I get married," and new recipes we'd try with fresh peaches tomorrow. And so few tomorrows were left . . .

I looked at another picture. It was crazy, but I thought about our trip to Kansas when I was fourteen. Just Mom and me.

"There's a Dairy Queen in one mile!" I announced.

I hopped out of the car at the little Dairy Queen order window. When the owner stuck his head under the window screen to take my order, it slipped down and trapped him! I turned away and watched my mother laughing in the car. I got the giggles as the man lifted the window. (He didn't find anything particularly funny about the incident, which made it all the more hysterical for us.) Unsuccessfully stifling chuckles, I ordered two hot fudge sundaes. Still no smile from the man.

When I got to the car, I found Mom doubled in gales of uncontrollable laughter. We laughed for twenty-five more miles.

More pictures, deep in the drawer. Who were these relatives? Why were these pictures important enough to save and haul through a dozen moves? I wonder. Did these people love my mom? I'll bet they did. But who were they? Where did they live? How did they intersect her life and where are they now?

It's funny. These questions are important to me now. Even Mom's dishes and linens in my cupboards now are important. Where did they come from? What was the link? Questions that weren't important five years ago. I just assumed answers then. But today I wonder. How I want to fit the pieces together!

Mother. Pushing daily with her last energy. Making a home. Wanting love so desperately for all of us.

My mother wasn't merely a friend. She was me. Today I see *her* when I walk by the mirror. I hear her voice when I talk.

I have so much living to do. How I wanted her to be a part of it. I held her picture and spoke my regret out loud: "Mother, I never knew you . . . enough."

Brokenness

"Käaren! I am your hostess here today and I want to do what you do! I want to write books and speak to vast crowds—even bigger than this! I can't talk now. I'm going to usher you to the front row and collect you after this session," a young woman bubbled as she took my arm. We were standing in the hallway of the church where I was to speak at a national singles' conference.

"Ah . . . that's great," I blurted, as she flashed a wide smile and swung around to leave. Her long, rich brown hair slapped across her flawless complexion. I doubted if she heard that I thought her goal was great. I doubted, too, that it would matter to her what I thought. Shelly knew what she wanted and in those few seconds she revealed enough about herself to convince me.

The opening session began with a rousing welcome from the conference coordinators. The auditorium was filled with hundreds of singles from around the country. The opening speaker began, but I was planning another speech—to Shelly. Often people wrote, called, or cornered me after meetings. They would say what Shelly said: "I want to write books and travel and speak." My mind went back to a woman who once pressed her name and address into my hand. "I want to be a writer. But I don't have any ideas," she pleaded.

"I don't mean to be flip, but why would you want to write, then?" I questioned. "Why toil and labor and build roads when you don't need them?"

Fall 1982

My thoughts flicked back to Shelly. *Ah, Shelly, my dear, dear, young beautiful woman,* I planned to say, *my dear, preppy young woman in your crisp navy Stanley Blacker blazer. So you want to write and speak. I want to expose you to reality. Writing often comes from brokenness, devastation, and pain that all level you on the ground with your insides falling out. I am sure that in your roughly thirty years you have not experienced much that merits listeners and readers. Oh, my dear, have you read Tozer? He said, "It's doubtful that God can use any man greatly until he's hurt him deeply." You can tell if speakers, writers, and ministers have been broken.*

Shelly, I continued mentally, *I know what it is to fall prostrate at my mother's grave. I know what it is to sit in restaurants alone and walk the streets of great cities around the world, struggling mentally and emotionally, holding onto faith by a frayed thread, believing that God would meet my deepest longings for a home and family when I was over thirty. I know what it is to find going home too painful.*

The opening session concluded. Shelly bucked the crowd and grabbed me again. Walking at a brisk clip through the hall to my seminar, she continued to rattle off her plans.

"I'll talk to you later," I said and smiled, patting her arm.

She gasped, squealed, and clapped her hands, then she raced on. I have never had such a glowing introduction as when Shelly then introduced me to the seminar. I told them, "I'm not sure she is talking about me, but after all, I see I *am* scheduled for this hall." Shelly sat in the front row and glowed. And empathized, seemingly.

Ah, she doesn't know how I feel. She couldn't possibly. Look at her, I insisted mentally as I was speaking. *She's just a good listener. A real charmer. My, this kid has savvy.*

I signed the last book, and Shelly and I were alone. Shelly began telling me, "I am a newborn Christian. I overheard a Christian witnessing to a man in a restaurant. I knew the man. I said to him, 'What is born again?' " She began fighting back tears. "Going home, I screamed in my car, 'Jesus Christ,

101

I want to be born again! I don't know exactly what it means. I want you in me—I'm asking. Ron said I could be born again just for the asking. This is all I know to do. I give you my life. This day! In this car! Cleanse me of my immoral past. Jesus Christ, I didn't know what was the gaping hole in my life: I had no spiritual dimension.'

"Käaren, you probably didn't know I had two husbands leave me. They were well known, successful men in this city. Talk about devastation . . . and that's only the beginning."

I gulped. "Shelly, I had no idea. You're so beautiful. Usually I see hundreds of miles of bad road across the faces of people who have had such experiences."

Shelly continued. "The whole side of my face is periodically paralyzed by a strange disorder called Bell's Palsy. Talk about humiliation and embarrassment. Your mouth is hanging open and the saliva is running out while you're talking, and you can't feel it! And my eyelid would droop . . ."

"Oh, Shelly," I responded, hoping she had never picked up my what-do-you-know-about-anything-Miss-Gorgeous attitude.

I changed my little speech to her. "You will bless the world. You will tell them he is a God who can be trusted. He is a God who forgives and reconstructs a life even through divorces and hideous circumstances."

"Well, of course, Käaren! I was born again!" she said in a matter-of-fact tone. We walked down the now-empty hall with our arms around each other.

"The Lord will use you greatly, I know." I smiled, squeezing her side.

New Year's Eve 1982

Couples . . . New Year's Eve

Having traveled to Oregon on professional business, I took the opportunity to visit my friends Tim and Nan. It happened to be New Year's Eve. I was staying at their house.

"We're going to go to a party. You are invited to join us," Nan announced.

"Great! What fun! A New Year's Eve party. I can't remember the last time I went to one! I usually watch Guy Lombardo reruns and eat chips and some unimaginative dip—which is anything with onion soup," I joked.

We laughed. Her laugh was in disbelief. Mine was to cover up.

Six couples made up the gathering. Six couples and me. The single. Over thirty. Never married. *What do they think about me?* I wondered. I decided not to flatter myself. They probably never gave me and my singleness a thought.

The hostess served things like Camembert and marinated mushrooms. There were conversations peppered with roaring male laughter in front of a massive, ceiling-height fireplace.

By 11:30 P.M. we decided to go around the room and share our goals for 1983. The couples were holding hands or curled in each others' arms, sitting deep in plush couches with enormous pillows. In a rocking chair with an afghan over my legs, I moved rhythmically.

By 11:45 P.M. I wanted to run. Inside I was dying emotionally. I felt trapped. *I don't have to be in such situations. I should have known better. I can be single and without a mate. I don't need this kind of painful reminder,* I screamed inwardly.

There were low lights, candles, and the moon on the Oregon mountains, which you could see through the all-glass walls of this opulent mountain home. Soon midnight would come. They would ring in the new year. I knew the couples would kiss each other. I decided I would smile and say, "How sweet," while churning and wrenching inside.

It's a pride thing, I know. But I didn't want them to feel sorry for me. I hoped they wouldn't remember I was single. I then began yelling inwardly statements such as, *These couples paid a big price for being curled up and cuddled. They've given up their freedom; they've had to submit to one another; they've had to bite their tongues, kill pride, and sacrifice—all that comes with being a couple. And you, Käaren Witte, have been able to travel the world, do radio and television, write books, and have a national ministry.*

But nothing eased the pain of the moment. No reality erased the hurt.

The wall clock chimed midnight.

In the stillness of the living room, in the glowing moonlight, each couple tenderly kissed, automatically tuning out the others. I pushed a smile on my face, as I had planned. Rocking steadily, I hoped to release some tension or absorb time.

Why can't I be a couple? The words hammered. I demanded them to stop. In stacatto they continued. *These women are just like me. Don't I too qualify for a quality husband like they each love?*

The couples wore winter plaids and cableknit sweaters. Red, seasonal clothes. Cuddly, huggable clothes. But then so did I.

The couples stopped kissing when the hostess announced the warm red Christmas punch. Everyone cheered. The intimate atmosphere was broken.

As I lay in the big guest bed later that night, I vowed I would always remember the single who sat alone.

"Jesus," I whispered in the night, "I won't forget the single. Because I won't forget New Year's Eve 1982."

Show me a great man or woman, someone who has enormous courage, someone of great compassion and empathy.

He or she has been through fires and black, frozen winters. — K.H.

Winter 1983

Men, Malls, and Tweedy Jackets

The whole world knows about a young man named Bruce Olson, who as a young college student braved the jungles of South America to reach a man-killing tribe, the Motilones, with the gospel. Bruce, formerly from Minnesota, decoded the Motilone language and translated the Bible into it. I had read about Bruce and often talked to some friends we had in common.

This week Bruce (who is close to my age) came to Tulsa to speak at my church. This was the first time I actually got to meet him! I videotaped an interview with him for a television special, "Every Single Day." When I picked him up at our pastor's house, I confessed, "Bruce, I'm intimidated by you. You are such a giant in the faith and so famous. I've been following your life for over fifteen years! Now you know how I feel about you. And I feel better having expressed it!"

He laughed for a full ten seconds.

I took him to a special French restaurant before the taping. He mentioned something he had read in *Opera News* and said he had subscribed to it in Colombia. I tried to project a casual and cool attitude that said, Well, doesn't everyone in the South American jungles subscribe to *Opera News?*

Later, while videotaping, I asked Bruce, "You devoted a chapter in your book *Bruchko* to Gloria, Bruce. You said she was your fiancée. Tell the viewers about Gloria."

"Gloria was killed in a car accident, as it says in the book," Bruce related unemotionally. "She was a beautiful woman. I loved her dearly."

One tear and you know what happens, Käaren Witte—a flood. Get control, I ordered myself. I admired his strength now more than ever.

After the taping Bruce wanted to shop in downtown Tulsa. We strolled through Williams Plaza, an elegant shopping center with shops circling an indoor ice skating rink.

I thought, *I'm well over thirty, but I don't ever recall shopping with a man. Leisurely shopping with a man. How unusual for me.*

"What a nice, polite, relaxed couple. Very nice people," I imagined the clerks and shopkeepers were saying about us or thinking as we milled in and out of their stores on that slow, quiet January afternoon.

So how did I come to this state in life with so little male companionship? I questioned myself inwardly, between chats with Bruce about American society and its merchandising mentality. I thought back. I had believed that if you want men to notice you, you should act cool. So I developed the attitude, "Buddy, if you want me . . . ah, MOI . . . to give you the time of day, you must come crawling. Because there is no way on God's green earth I'm going to get in the line for you with the rest of the uncool women! Never! I've got dignity and pride!"

You know what? Nobody came crawling. But today, I am happily "me" with men. If I am too outgoing, too demonstrative, too talkative, too gushy, then too bad! I'm just me. At last. *Now that's freedom,* I concluded mentally. My conversation with Bruce resumed.

My mind drifted again. I kept thinking, as we shopped and browsed, about how different our lives were—Bruce's and mine—from most people's. We were both single and past thirty. Bruce had been in the remotest jungle for over twenty years. And me? I had my own jungle. Struggling with the desire to be married all through my twenties, then

Flying Solo

resigning with faith only to find myself steeped in more singleness—as a career.

Both of us, I continued to ponder, were going it alone, following that different drummer for lofty dreams in life, yet remaining in the great fellowship of believers.

My thought this day was never, *Is Bruce a potential?* I simply believed the Lord arranged this day to assure me I was still a feeling woman who could appreciate and admire a great man.

Bruce proved something to me: that I could log time with one of the great leaders of the world and be interesting company for him.

How different my world is from that of most women, I continued to review mentally. *I wonder, will I ever contemplate waxy build-up and struggle at 4:30 P.M. with the great decision, "What's for supper?" Will I ever sort socks while watching reruns of "The Waltons," and think of laundry as an art form?*

This week I had met with Jesus early in the morning. I was prepared for today with Bruce. I had made a new commitment: "Jesus, whatever makes you happy, that's what I want to do."

I have it settled. Because I know Jesus is secretly planning behind the scenes.

For me. For you.

6:30 A.M. *Daily*

The first thing I do every day is slip out of bed
    and immediately bend down on my knees.
I say Galatians 3:20.
I pray, "Put a watch over my mouth. I want this day to
    glorify you."
Today I also prayed: "Live out victory in my life, Jesus. The
    miracle will not necessarily be the answered prayers,
      but the changing
        of me."

My Awesome Responsibility

"I married Jack, Käaren, because I didn't believe in this wait-for-God's-best business. I didn't believe there was such a thing. I didn't care that he wasn't the greatest Christian on earth. I was lonely! I was thirty years old. I desperately longed for a companion and husband," a young woman going through throes of divorce choked and cried at my desk. "Why did God let me marry this jerk?"

"Linda, we do have a choice," I responded softly.

"Oh, I know," she said regretfully.

Linda left my office, and I buried my head in my arms. "Jesus, oh, why not me? You rescued and saved me from men like Jack—Linda's choice. I still must make choices. Guide me!"

How responsible I am for this life of mine, for my choice of a life's mate, I thought. *My dear dad and mom . . . how they sacrificed for me. Dad working two jobs in the early days and later building businesses that cost him his blood. And Mother, working with Dad on the books, the selling, over long days that bled into months and years. They gave their lives for me so I could attend the best schools, travel, buy clothes and cars.*

Passing their bedroom in the early morning, I would hear Dad and Mom pray, "God, thank you for our sweet girl. Thank you for the patience and grace you've shown through her doubtings. God, we know you promised miracles and opportunities in our daughter's life. Our dreams for her beautiful little life are great and glorious. We know they can be! You, God, are making them happen. We're partners with you, in the future of our girl. And oh, God, give her a kind man. Lead them together in your supernatural way. Flood her with grace in the waiting."

How they must love me to get on their knees in the early morning, I'd think.

I'm beginning to realize all they invested in me. It helps me begin to get a glimpse of what Jesus did for me. He gave his lifeblood, his dreams, his goals, his achievements, his desires, his ambitions, his pride, his reputation, so that little girls from plain towns separated by miles of flat, unimaginative land could live out their dreams. Great lives could be theirs, full of goals, achievements, fame, and a sense of pride and fulfillment.

Dad worked two jobs and later ran three businesses so that I could have braces, go to the skin doctors, and travel to New York to see Broadway (very heady for kids in rural Minnesota in the late sixties). He loved me enough not to let me be a waitress even at the "fun restaurant" in town, where all the kids hung out, because they wanted me to work one Sunday a month. He loved me enough to see me hurt when he wouldn't let me date Ron Ettleman. It didn't matter that Ron was a basketball player and had an enviable muffler on his '58 Ford. Dad saw a lack of "character qualities." (Twenty years later, I saw what Dad saw. Ron didn't exactly become a fine husband and father, to say the least.)

"But Dad, I'm not going to marry Ron! Can't I go to the hockey game with him?" I'd plead.

"Honey, he's not what I dream for you," he'd say, touching my face with one hand and looking grieved.

I'd think about it at the time. *I do respect his opinion, God. I know Dad loves me and sacrifices for me. But what if no one else ever comes along?*

Today I live alone, twenty-three floors above the earth. I have no bedrooms to pass and hear praying parents interceding for me on their knees. "Oh, Jesus Christ, I am so responsible for my life. I must make the right choices," I now pray on my knees in the early mornings beside my own big bed. "I will sacrifice, no matter what it costs me. Look at what you and my parents have invested in me. I can't do anything less. I will wait and wait for God's man. Your first choice. It's the least I can do."

"But Käaren, you're well into your thirties. You can't be so fussy. The kind of man you are holding out for just doesn't exist," Melanie, a thirty-five-year-old, twice-divorced friend insisted just yesterday in my women's Bible study. "I've got a guy for you to meet. You two are a perfect match!"

"But Melanie, I must wait. I could not hurt those who gave their lifeblood for me!"

"Yes, you do have a beautiful life," Melanie conceded.

"Melanie, I just can't date indiscriminately. I just can't marry quickly and thoughtlessly. Jesus Christ and my parents have too much at stake in my life!" I pressed, holding her hand in mine.

"But Käaren, you may never meet the kind of man we all know you're holding out for," she continued, insisting.

"So be it. I can't do anything less for those who kill themselves and give their lives for me," I affirmed. "Melanie, Jesus has invested just as much in you, and you can trust him for a great Christian mate! Please wait and trust and believe with me," I pleaded. "I need you to believe with me."

"I'll try. I want to. I really want to sense a great indebtedness to Jesus Christ, too, even down to choosing a mate. Yes, Käaren, I will wait with you, for you, for me," she pledged and then held me tightly.

Will you wait with me? I will wait with you.

New Job: Church Singles' Director

"How's the new job going?" a friend inquired after my first week.

"Today," I answered, "there were thirteen phone calls. Five asked, 'Where are all the men?' Six asked, 'Why doesn't God give me a mate?' And two said, 'I don't have anything to live for.'"

Loneliness

Loneliness—a universal problem, but it seems Americans know it best.

Qualities I valued in a young man when I was sixteen: wearing a letter jacket, knowing all the words to the song "Yesterday," and playing three chords on a guitar.

I pray about my loneliness when it hits. But God is faithful, showing me how to remedy it.

I remember living in a house with two other young single women from my church. Each Sunday morning one housemate would say, "I'm going to drive separately, Käaren, because you always talk to people afterward. I don't want to hang around for ten or fifteen minutes."

"And, Becky, I'm not going to ride with you because you leave the house ten minutes before you actually have to," the other would announce.

"I guess I'll drive separately, too. Then I don't have to bend for anyone either!" I'd proclaim.

So we'd take three separate cars to church. Then we three would each drive to lunch and then drive home alone.

This small story makes a revealing comment about us: No one was willing to sacrifice and bend for the others. We were selfish, independent—and we wondered why we experienced so much loneliness.

Here at my church where I am now singles' director we have one large photocopying machine. Sometimes it's necessary to wait a few seconds, or maybe three or four minutes, while someone runs something off.

I used to fuss in my head, *Why can't this big-budgeted church swing another copy machine! I don't want to waste time waiting.*

Now when I race to the little copier room, I smile, especially if someone is using the machine. It makes for a few peaceful moments in my pushed and pressured life to simply be alone with one of my "family members."

I smile and say a personal word. I offer a blessing on their behalf to the Father. "Jesus, do something warm and touching for Mary today," I pray silently, while Mary tells me her holiday plans or how her cold is progressing.

I love the little unsuspecting ways God provides to meet all my needs, including social ones.

He is God—if I let him be.

Spring 1983

The Deep Need

Today I had surgery on my face. A small benign tumor was removed from the side of my nose. And I discovered—uncovered—a need in me. A need deep and buried.

The plastic surgeon often held my shoulders and arms during the surgery. His concern and compassion were healing to me.

"Does this hurt?" he'd often ask.

"No," I always responded. But it did hurt. It was especially excruciating as the needles pushed long and deep into sensitive facial tissue.

Why did I say it didn't hurt?

Because it just felt so good to be close to another human being.

Doesn't it say something about my need—our need—for close human contact, when being cut in the face is the price? (And it didn't seem like a big price.)

Lying on my bed afterward, I petitioned, *Oh, Jesus. Father God. Sir. You know my great need. Yes, I have chosen to follow you. Yes, a thousand times yes. I will sacrifice my needs to follow you. I promise to follow you no matter what the cost. But, Jesus, I know you are arranging a mate for me. Someone to hold me. I know I can make it through days like this—bandages on my face, the throbbing pain, and the stillness of the apartment broken only by a barking dog and thud of the afternoon paper hitting the door. There is an end, a light at the end of this tunnel, too. You will provide strong, caring arms for Käaren. Someday. Some way.*

One day I will say, "Oh, Jesus Christ! Now I understand! Now I see! It's so perfectly clear why you had me be single all these years. You never waste a moment, an experience, an opportunity, a contact, in the lives of your children!"

But for now, Jesus, reach down and meet my deepest need and longing this moment.

Nobody's Child

"Where are the chocolate chips, please?" I asked the grocery store clerk.

"Right this way, aisle five," he answered, skipping down the aisle with me. "I'll bet you're going to make cookies for your husband and kiddoes!" he said.

"Ah . . . something like that," I answered, forcing a smile.

So what am I supposed to say? I interrogated myself. *"My kids? My husband? Well, Mr. Employee, I don't have either."* Then let him scan me over and try to figure out why I didn't belong to anybody. *Skip it.*

The trouble was I couldn't skip it. Something triggered old, well-remembered pain to the surface to haunt me again. I continued to think, aimlessly pushing my cart down the next aisle, and the next, *I want to belong to somebody. Please, Jesus, hear my heart today on aisle seven.*

In my third grade Sunday school class, some of my classmates came from a local children's home.

"Who's child are you?" a church worker asked one of those homeless little girls.

"I'm nobody's child," she answered, bowing her head.

I remember "Nobody's Child." Her name was Ellen. Empty eyes. Cropped hair. Loveless face. Bony little body. Functional, but always too-big dress in dark plaid. Dusty brown shoes. No mother to put ribbons in her curls. No Daddy to tickle her tummy just to hear her giggle.

"Nobody's child"—that's what I felt like at that moment.

But what I felt is a lie. The promise is "it is the Father's great pleasure to give Käaren the kingdom" (Luke 12:32).

I choose faith, one more time. I cling to it tenaciously.

The faith I flood my mind and heart with in aisle seven is for the dream—a lush valley of green—that will come forth from the barren, dry land watered only by my tears as I walk alone.

Summer 1983

Someone Waiting Just for Me

"Let him find you!" I instructed another auditorium of singles regarding mating, at yet another singles' conference. Then I boarded a plane home.

"Tell Grady to pick me up," I had schemed with my friend Dan as he drove me to the airport to attend the conference.

"Oh, good idea! After all, it's a legitimate need. And remember, I continually told you: 'Need men, too, Käaren.' You know how it looks: You don't need anybody!"

"Well, I need now! Plus Grady knows my car's in the repair shop," I gleefully answered, relishing the opportunity.

Grady. A strong, hulking man. One of the most talented, sincerest men in ministry. He traveled full-time in a ministry combining music and speaking. We had shared the platform on several occasions. We "flowed." Comments ranged from "a team" to "You two are a dynamic duo!"

"Spectacular," one man commented on his piano playing at a concert.

"Anointed, deep, sensitive," another said about his speaking.

"He'll go far. God will honor his pure motives. You watch. In five years the whole world will know him," I predicted to friends.

His reserve, I decided, was, well, because he was a male, less verbal than we women, and perhaps he was shy. His personal life remained private. "Just give him time. He'll open up to you," I assured myself.

Prior to boarding my return flight from the conference, I invested one hour in my appearance at the airport—redoing my makeup, plying the curling iron, and changing outfits in the washroom.

"You're going to something special! You're sure not going home!" the washroom attendant laughed, as she mopped around me.

I smiled at her. My secret. I returned the laugh.

I usually hop a cab and slip back into my apartment, I thought, my head on an airline pillow. *How different this flight is from hundreds of others. No working on the week's schedule. No outlines for book chapters. No notes for seminars. No "to do" lists. Not this time.*

Just relax and stay fresh. Check the mascara before I land. A satisfied smile played on my face. *Tonight, somebody's planning to meet me. I'll be like these other homebound passengers who get met by loved ones at airports.*

I wonder. Does it get to the businessmen when, flight after flight, nobody meets them? I suppose not. One gets jaded, robotic, about flights and airports. I know.

But tonight was different. Tonight belonged to me. I had watched many pretty girls with little smiles across their unlined faces. For they would be met. They owned the future. They knew it. Love and strong arms awaited. The fulfillment of feminine destiny.

And me? At last some of that feminine destiny would be fulfilled for me too—tonight.

Johnny Mathis sang "Chances Are" in my head, a song that had played on the radio one night when Grady stopped over for coffee.

I giggled out loud.

"Just tell Grady to meet me at the luggage carousel. No need to park in the lot or ramp," I instructed Dan.

I know the caliber of this man. He will park in the ramp and be right there at the gate, I judged mentally, knowing his impeccable manners and gracious manliness.

I sat gingerly so as not to wrinkle my dress—a girlish summer frock with a ruffled collar and a matching bow for my hair. How crisp and feminine I felt in my white flats and light-colored hose.

"I like your outfit," one stewardess affirmed, as she raced down the aisle with magazines.

I turned the overhead air conditioning on full blast. I didn't want my skin to even get clammy, let alone SWEAT. Shivering, I thought, *Freezing is a small sacrifice.*

The moment arrived. The plane touched down.

The waiting area teemed with people.

Summertime travelers, I concluded. *Grady is here, somewhere.* I scanned the crowd, searching for his towering head with its black, curly hair.

The luggage—he'll be there, I reassured myself.

I waited, watching couples young and old. Arm in arm. Hugging. Holding. Helping. But any minute I would have a big hug and a very nice man lifting my suitcases and smiling at me. With me.

One hour passed. Darkness came. The airport windows made a mirror. As I watched cars stop and pick up passengers, I studied my reflection and thought—no, agonized.

Am I not pretty enough? Too fat? Can't size ten cut it in today's relentlessly thinness-demanding society? Am I not giving, sensitive enough? Am I not woman enough? Soft and sweet enough? Am I too old now for even men my age? Are they at the stage when only younger women will do? Now it didn't matter about my mascara. Tears warmed, then cooled, my tanned cheeks.

There was an explanation, I was certain. But the old phrase I'd told many, "We have time for who we want to have time for," rolled through my weary head. I moved outside and motioned to a cab. We drove out of the airport.

"Oh! There's Grady," I exclaimed to the driver. "Yes, that's his car! Follow that car!"

Back through the arrival entrance and to the loading zone we sped.

"No, that isn't the car," I admitted to the driver.

Then came the long drive through the downtown Tulsa night. My thoughts were moving slowly now. Dulling pain does that.

I thought I quit having unrealistic expectations when I was a college student, I ruefully thought to myself. *Professional women my age just don't have times like this.*

Grady was in concert the following night. I had planned for weeks to go and bring friends. He called that afternoon but made no reference to the airport.

My girlfriends and I arrived at the concert. Hope lived. I had washed the same ruffled dress and freshened the bow. I glowed. A year easily blends into the next without meeting someone so unusual, so rare and God-centered, as Grady.

Oh, God, don't let him see us, I prayed as we walked through the huge doors of the concert hall.

You must look at him. To ignore would be obvious. Wave! I commanded my crying heart.

Grady, posing at a flowered, grassy fountain area, embraced a beautiful young woman as a photographer snapped pictures.

Inside the auditorium the same young woman sat in the front row. Alone. He played to her and their eyes locked at brief moments during the concert. Autographing records afterwards, he used the word "fiancée" as he hugged her and others gathered around the much-loved star.

"When will it ever be lucky me . . . ," the song hammered in my head.

I won't let on to my friends, I determined mentally. And I didn't. We all went out for the proverbial coffee. Somebody in the group mentioned the beautiful girl with Grady at the autograph table.

"I heard he was getting married," one announced.

"They looked like it!" I said, feigning rejoicing.

I hope I was a good actress at that moment. I needed to cover the results of my unrealistic expectation—humiliation, defeat, and depression—one more time. But the last time, I promised God. And myself.

How to Be Beautiful Without Being Good-Looking

"Good grief! Who's this man? Whatever happened to him? He looks awful," Julie exclaimed, studying a small framed photo on my living room end table. "What happened to his face? Why doesn't he get some help? There's a lot that can be done in cosmetic surgery today."

I remained silent.

"Well, don't you agree? This guy is horrible looking," Julie insisted.

"Julie, I don't see him as horrible or ugly. I see him as—"

"Oh, come on, all the good-looking people you know . . . Are you kidding me? You can't possibly think this guy is decent looking," Julie interrupted.

I told her about the man in the photo: Merrill Womach. "He is a famous gospel singer and he was in a plane crash. His entire face was burned off. Through hundreds of painful, excruciating operations, his face was rebuilt."

"Oh. I didn't know," Julie apologized, lowering her head and returning the photo to the table.

"Julie, I followed Merrill's story when I first heard about the plane crash. I then read his book *Tested by Fire* and attended his concerts. I even corresponded with him. How I admired him! I often thought to myself, what a courageous, internally strong man. He will never give up in his life's dream of singing for Christ! What fortitude he has, what real character. What a man. And Julie, that's what being a man really is—courage, determination, forbearance. That's what macho is about, not gold chains and Gucci loafers," I pressed, alternating looking at the picture and clutching it to my chest.

"I understand why you admire him, Käaren," Julie whispered, putting her hand on my shoulder in that sensitive moment. "Any man who looks like this and goes through life with a public career is to be admired."

"Julie, when I met Mr. Womach I asked to have his picture taken with me," I recalled, "but the instant after I asked him I panicked! I wondered, Does a man who's so scarred and deformed ever want his picture taken?"

The moment I asked him, he smiled, put his arm around my shoulders, and posed for the photographer. Before he left, he took my two hands in his and held them firmly. His eyes poured into mine. He was touching my soul as he put my anxious heart to rest. His spirit proclaimed to mine, "It's okay, Käaren! Everything is settled. I'm at peace. It's all okay by me."

When a smile surfaced and a light came to my eyes, he was convinced. He waited. He kept holding my hands until he knew. I believed him.

My hands returned his warm squeeze.

As he walked away after those incredibly emotional moments, I said to the photographer, "There goes a real man. How I admire him. And there goes one of the most handsome, gorgeous men I will ever meet. He has such a vision, a dream, a drive, a purpose. A purpose so great that even having his face burned off will not stop him."

I have had other, similar lessons about what makes a person beautiful and attractive.

I remember one house I lived in after college, with six other young women. Every night someone would have a date. Any of those still awake when they returned got the recap and review of the man.

A consistent thread ran through those conversations. We would hear either "Oh, he doesn't know where he's going in life. He just doesn't have any direction, goals, or ideas," or "Wow! This guy has a burn and vision. He's a go-getter. He is making his life count. I'm so attracted to him and his dream!"

Never once did the girls initially discuss their dates' looks.

When I was speaking in the Midwest recently, a striking young man, thirtyish, sat in the front row. He was tall, lean, and golden blond. Ivy League clothes. His perfect appearance had one flaw. He wore one black sock and one brown. I wondered.

His designer glasses were tinted. (I just wrote it off as being part of his "cool.") During my speech, he only looked at me once. I wondered why.

"Are there any questions or comments?" I asked the audience after speaking on "How to Be Beautiful Without Being Good-Looking."

"Käaren, I have one." The young man in the front row stood and waited until the auditorium was silent. "I am blind. I've been blind due to kidney failure for two years. But don't pity me. A wonderful thing has happened. You see, I was a male model and actor. I would go to singles' gatherings and groups and only approach the best-looking women. I was repulsed by anyone over thirty or overweight. Different people from my church tried to fix me up with women. Once I left a double date—I had never met the young woman—because the other couple who arranged the date neglected to tell me she was fifteen pounds overweight and over thirty—plus I had always hated those little crow's feet around women's eyes.

"And when different greeters and friendly women in groups approached," he continued before a mesmerized crowd, "I'd walk away without saying anything or leave them in mid-sentence if they weren't gorgeous. 'Shoot, I don't have to put up with these scruffy lookin' women,' I'd think to myself or maybe even declare to another person.

"No, don't pity my blindness," he continued. "This is the best thing that ever happened to me. Because today every human being I speak to, I *really see*. I see their displays of love. I see their times of sacrificing for one another. I see their enormous compassion and concern for one another. To me, you are all beautiful." The audience was weeping.

I don't remember what shallow little words I sputtered out to dismiss the audience that evening, but I do remember the embracing and the freely flowing tears.

I got in line to hug the blind, handsome young man. I knew that this exquisitely good-looking man would never think one negative thing about my appearance. He said he thought we all were beautiful. And I believed him.

Then there was Duane.

Duane was an arrogant, critical single in my singles' group. He drove us up the wall with his pseudo-Harvard, café-literati language.

We all avoided Duane. Except for Joe. Joe began meeting Duane daily at 5:00 A.M. for prayer and Bible study in the parking lot of a quick-stop store. Duane became humble, warm, loving, and encouraging, within three weeks!

We knew that Joe had stepped out from the pack of us who had written Duane off. And it wasn't as if Joe didn't have anything else to do but hang around the quick-stop at 5:00 A.M.! He is a successful surgeon. He could have spent time with the most brilliant, sophisticated, sought-after people. But he didn't. He chose the unlovable.

It's a funny thing. When I first met Joe I didn't find him physically attractive. But as I've seen him sacrifice and give his life, I have begun to see him as handsome. He's a beautiful person. I'd be delighted to meet with him at the quick-stop at 5:00 A.M. any day.

"Is love only for the beautiful or the lucky, Käaren?" A twenty-nine-year-old single, never-married woman cried as she sat in my office. "I learned early in life—we all did—that love is only for clear-skinned girls with perfect adolescent bodies. I overheard one girl say about another (and secretly I knew she was right), 'Lynn married a handsome, successful man. In fact, he is very well off, and we always knew Lynn would marry well because she was so beautiful.'

"Käaren," the woman in my office continued, "will some good man, not some jerk, ever accept me and love me?"

"Yes," I said. We then talked for an hour about "looks." I told her the story of Michele from my second book, *Great Leaps in a Single Bound*.

One of the most handsome, glowing Christian men I ever met spent a day ushering me from one bookstore to another when my first book was released. Between autographing books, I picked this guy's brain. I probed and questioned him. What kind of girls did he ever date anyway? What kind of woman did he eventually marry? Who would qualify for this outstanding, brilliant, physically gorgeous man?

At the end of the day, this young man invited me to join him and his new wife for dinner. When she approached the table I begged God, *Oh, please, don't let that be her. And if it is, please don't let my face betray me. She mustn't read any shock on my face. She's suffered, I'm sure, intense emotional pain.*

Michele had a disfigured face. I guessed burns. I knew I was overacting to appear unaffected and cheery. And she knew it.

Michele was angelically kind. Her warm, loving eyes burned into mine as I spoke. Our souls became bonded as I shared my hurts with her. She cared deeply as I talked about my struggles with singleness, with all the longings for a home and family. Her enormous brown eyes filled with tears. Her courage for herself and me kept them from overflowing.

Michele related her story: "Käaren, I never dated in college or high school. I always believed God allowed my burn accident for a great statement in my life, and I intended to build a dream out of my life. I knew I could, simply because I followed Jesus. I chose to believe with all my heart that God had a very special plan for my life. I knew I would have total trust and lived in glowing anticipation for a wonderful Christian mate. And Käaren, you'll have to agree, God did honor my faith and give me a wonderful mate."

I agreed!

I saw what a beautiful person Michele had become through her love and great faith. (So had her husband!)

Psychologist James Dobson has spoken about the emphasis we place on physical attractiveness in our country. He says it is the by-product of the sexual revolution, which has erotically supercharged our culture. Today there is an unparalleled fascination with sex, he reports, and when sex becomes paramount in people's lives, they will value good looks. Hence Christian singles often

I choose life — maximum life, not short-term gratification.

                                                   KgL

"Good looks may open the door, but they don't hold it open."

Rob Schmidt, M.D.

choose mates and dates using this *foolish measure* of human worth!

Let us not mistake charisma for character, or showmanship for anointing, either! Let us not be dating Christians with all the earmarks of the world. And let us see how we become beautiful to others: when we love them and sacrifice for them.

Just Joking

"Käaren, do you know what the singles' breakfast special is?" a friend in my singles' ministry asked.

"No," I answered.

"It's a microwaved burrito at the Get 'n Go quick-stop before 7:00 A.M.," he snickered.

Forgiveness

"God can't forgive me. I've had several affairs with married men, and I've slept with at least five other men," a petite, twenty-six-year-old single sobbed in my office.

"I feel so alone, so abandoned. I'm devastated emotionally and psychologically," she continued, trembling.

Again I showed her I John 1:9 in the New Testament, which promises that if we confess our sins God is faithful to forgive them.

"When you refuse to accept forgiveness, you are rising above God. *You* are making the rules and conditions. Please stop saying what God can or cannot forgive. He sets the conditions for sin and forgiveness, not you," I pleaded, walking around the desk to hold her in my arms.

She promised she would accept forgiveness. And she has.

Observations

Before we marry, we must determine our prospective mate's behavior and character. We must see how the other handles pressure, adversity, and tough testing.

Anything less is a gamble.

Lies

All the good ones are gone. (No they're not. They're just in the making—editorial comment.)
You're just too fussy. (*Au contraire.* You'd be surprised what starts lookin' good after thirty—editorial comment.)

You must be turning men off.

You're better off single.

When are you going to settle down? (So what does "settle down" mean anyway?—editorial comment.)

If you don't meet a mate in college, you might as well forget it.

You're over twenty-nine now, you'll never get married. You're too set in your ways.

The School of Patience

Are you currently enrolled in God's "School of Patience"? Moses learned patience in the desert as he tended sheep. Unknown to him, God was using those years as part of a tailor-made program to prepare Moses for shepherding a much larger flock—the emerging nation of Israel. Only when Moses was *truly ready* did God appear to him in the burning bush and send him back to Egypt.

God's patience-building process may seem *agonizingly* slow to you, but remember, your response to God's tutoring is all-important. How fast are you learning the lessons you need to master in order to be ready for greater service when he calls?

Dear Lord, because I know you want to use me in a significant way, please help me to learn the lesson in patience you have set before me today.

Olympics

"Are you going to watch the Winter Olympics? The ice skating, the skiing, the sliding, the sledding?" a friend in Tulsa asked.

"In Minnesota we called that going to work every day!" I laughed.

I Want to Be a Couple; or, Fed Up with Singles

Today I wanted to be a couple. I wanted to be a part of the coupled world.

I ached to do things as a couple, with other couples. Dinners. Tennis. I wondered what must it be like vacationing with another couple, joking about "the gals always being late" and "men hating shopping." Stuff that nobody takes seriously but just uses as endearment material.

One of the pastors on my staff brought his wife, Linda, to a singles' party.

Could I please be your friends, just for tonight? Could I belong to you? Could I think of myself as a couple for just this one night? Could we act like we have been couples before in social situations? Could we make a statement to the singles by eating together, chatting, and laughing? I begged them mentally as I watched them entering.

I watched the couple. My friends. As good friends as possible without it being awkward, I guess.

He would introduce her to the singles with his arm around her. She would be soft and demure. He paved the way for her socially.

What do friendships require of a single? I had often quizzed myself, and now I asked, What would Tim and Linda say about me?

They would say, Sure, I was their friend. Tim pats me on the back and says he appreciates and admires my singles' ministry. Linda warms me with smiles and compliments me on weight loss.

What's the balance to be sought, in being friends with couples? Do I primarily talk a lot with Linda? Do I try to be cooler with Tim because I don't want Linda to feel left out or threatened? My old questions surfaced yet another time.

I've learned never to laugh at any married man's jokes too much. I don't get too enthralled with his words, ideas, job, and hobbies. I limit the "Wows," the "Tell me mores," and comments like "How interesting."

Some moments I cringe at my feelings. People would be surprised if they knew how a singles' director thinks—and prays.

"Jesus, I am relegated to the singles because I am a single. Oh, if I were a basket case some marrieds would take me in, take me under their wings. But I'm not. So my close associations must be with singles, people who are so often broken and banged-up emotionally—especially after thirty. Often they have had a tragic divorce (what divorce isn't tragic?) multiple marriages, children. Jesus, can't I have a close friendship with people who build strong homes and great marriages and outstanding families? People who don't have axes to grind, ex-mates to sabotage, bitterness and disillusionment reflected in their words? I long to be with achievers, accomplished goal setters, beautifully confident and exquisitely mannered people!"

You know what Jesus answered?

"I could have had the company and fellowship of the exquisitely schooled, the beautifully confident and elegantly mannered, too. But I chose you, Käären Witte. I did it so you might become the exquisite human being I dreamed you'd become".

I prayed again.

"Thank you, Jesus, for singles. They help me get a glimmer of understanding of you, of your love, of how you relate to me." I repented.

One more time.

Verily I Say, the "Harolds" Shall Always Be with Us!

"Hey! You're really funny!" I laughed as one new man in my singles' group joked at the punch bowl.

"You wanna get married?" he jumped, erasing the smile from his face and pumping a wild handshake.

"Ah, Harold," I demurred, reading his name tag, "I make it a policy to at least go out for coffee before making any major decisions in life."

"Oh. I suppose that means you'd need a refill, too."

Smile. Laugh. It feels good.

Where Credit's Due

A five-year dream realized: hosting and producing my own daily talk show for singles called "Every Single Day."

I slipped a sheet of paper to the men in the control room. The credits were typed on it.

"Käaren Witte's clothes and jewelry courtesy of Al Witte," the credits read as they rolled by at the end of the program each day. Viewers began calling and asking, "Where's 'Al Witte' located?"

Puzzled, the station management reviewed the credits.

"Come clean, Witte. You tried to slip this through," my executive producer *sort of* joked.

"Okay, okay. 'Käaren Witte's clothes and jewelry courtesy of Al Witte,' as you read on the credits each day . . . ah, okay. So . . . Al Witte is my dad!" I confessed to the viewers, feigning remorse. After all, I wanted to give credit to Dad, who *did* fund all those clothes for many years!

God, help me to be more concerned about getting to know this young man than concerned about falling in love.

                                      KJ

People Make a Marriage

I think I know about *getting* married. But I certainly don't know about *being* married.

I heard someone say: "Divorce doesn't work. You divorce a sinner, but if you remarry, you marry a sinner."

Another said, "It's never marital problems people have; it's personal problems."

A Real Man . . . in the Dating System

Mollie and Rich broke their engagement this year. She entered the Miss America pageant. He is a television talk-show host. A movie star look-alike—tanned, tall.

Last night after church Mike, a handsome new man in our fellowship, asked Rich, "Who was that young lady with you earlier?"

"Come on! I want you to meet her!" Rich encouraged, pulling Mike's arm and moving toward Mollie.

"It's only been a few months since the broken engagement," I thought, wincing for Rich and Mollie. Maybe they both were still in the wake of their emotional hurt.

I detest our culture's dating system. Is it biblical? I questioned mentally as I watched the scene unfold.

Other questions flashed by me in that instant. *This system is based on accepting or rejecting. I don't want to reject anybody. And I don't want to be rejected. We use words like "breaking up." We are talking about human beings for whom Jesus Christ died, flesh and blood human beings with feelings. How dare we "break" each other?*

I felt jolted when I observed Rich introducing Mike to Mollie.

"Rich," I began the next morning on the phone, "I watched the whole thing last night."

"What thing?"

"I watched you introduce another man to Mollie."

"I want the best for her," he answered, with a trace of emotion in his voice. "I know God will bless me for it. And I want to become all God wants and dreams."

"Rich, it takes a real man to do what you did. A big man. I admire you." I was now connecting to him with my own thread of emotion. "It takes a real man in today's world to identify with the most controversial figure in all of history—Jesus Christ. And you not only identify with him but you treat others—in the toughest of situations—as Jesus would."

"Thank you, Käaren," he said.

We hung up. I put my head on the phone. I cried about the horrible impacts we have on one another so often in this dating system.

"God, I want to be a real woman. A strong, great Christian woman. One who would have the courage to say to someone—even if it means dateless Fourth of July weekends and New Year's Eves—'I care about you. Your very soul. I will not treat your emotions and personhood as if I were flicking a stray thread off my coat.' And God, I know you will bring someone into my life. Someone with whom I could build something strong and real. And together we'll soar, dreaming about making a difference with our lives. I never want to break another soul or to be broken again myself. I trust you, God, to lead us together so we may avoid the wrenching aftermath of the dating system. And thank you, God, for Rich. A real man. Your man."

I Haven't Been Truthful About Me

Dear Jesus,
Make me real.
Make me authentic.
Put your search light on my pretense.
I hate it.
And you hate it.
I want to be a genuine Christian
   Not faking

Not hiding critical attitudes and bitterness.
I hate my pride that makes me want to have other speakers think
I'm "sought after" and "in demand."
The pride that hides thoughts and begs, "Why little ol' me? I'd never have such negative or lustful thoughts!"
That pride that juggles numbers to let others believe my books outsell every book in the world.
That ugly pride that lies (and everybody knows it) as it sniffs "Oh, I could have been married many times. There have been lots of opportunities."
The jealousy and self-pity I feel over someone younger when I walk into a $200,000 house belonging to someone just twenty six years old.
I allow you, Jesus, to pull back the curtain and let me see the *me* you and I long for. *Me*: pure and honest before the world. The *me* I cry out to be.
I invite you.
Reveal my motives.
I know I can't be perfect.
But I can be real.
I want to be real. Without pretense.
Because I haven't been.
And the coverup has been an impossible burden.

My Soul Sings 3

Spring 1984

Looking Back, Looking Ahead, on Marriage

"I'm looking forward to getting married! I will take piano lessons, tennis lessons, and practice my guitar. I won't have to work! I'll write books and news stories. I'll sew. I'll travel with my mate. My biggest decision of the day will be where to take our lunch—my girlfriends and me! I'll cruise about the shopping centers and quaint restaurants in a car provided courtesy of my wonderful, hardworking hubby, who, of course, will handle all maintenance! (My, those oil changes and repairs are a bore!)" I stated, without questioning reality or motives as I sat with my college roommates.

Today I see what marriage is—in one word: sacrifice. In one idea: Help your husband get what he wants in life.

How awesome to take another life and invest your heart and blood in him! Helping him become all God dreams for him. Nothing less. To intercede in long hours of prayer, extending your faith for him, believing in him when he falls into black holes of depression, and visualizing outrageous dreams for him. Dreams with worldwide influence—nothing less.

Today my goal is not motivated by what marriage may provide: the house, the finances, the partner, opportunities for me. I'm beginning to understand that marriage is a mind-boggling commitment. My mate will be putting his life into my heart and hands. He will trust, and risk, his life.

"Jesus, my hope and helper, with grace and help I will be

that woman behind the man. The man the whole will know. God, I'm depending on you to put a searchlight on me, my heart and motives. I must kill selfishness. Because even with my lofty talk, I still have that human nature which connives to get something for nothing, that nature which begs to be noticed. That strives to be a somebody. That screams for attention, strokes, and applause continually," I pray.

This prayer and my acting on the hope and help of Jesus will make all the difference, in my life and in his.

You're Next

Another close friend got married today.
A storybook romance—everyone said so.
Four hundred people attended the reception.
The bouquet toss and garter toss got under way late. Most of the wedding-goers had left—except for the singles. We tend to leave most things last. Why rush home?

I had been brave. I smiled and congratulated, talked to everybody I knew and introduced myself to those I didn't.

Pretty gracious and decent for a single "never-been married" in her mid-thirties facing another mid-thirty single "never-been" friend getting married. To a beautiful man.

I stood far on the side of the group for the bouquet toss.

"They would kill puppies to catch the bouquet," one married man howled. He proceeded to laugh himself into a choking fit while sipping his punch.

When the bride lifted her arm, the tight sleeve locked her elbow. The bouquet went askew, right to the outer limits of the squealing group of single women.

If I hadn't reached for it, it would have hit me in the face. There I stood looking down at white and pink roses nestled in baby's breath. Everyone applauded and yelled, "You're next."

They've been saying "You're next" at every wedding and shower for fifteen years. I'm never next, I protested mentally.

I threw it back.

The Freedom Factor

Amanda cried while curled up on my living room couch.
There is one basic tenet in human nature we shouldn't violate: freedom.

The grass may be greener on the other side of the fence but everybody mows!

Amanda violated a young man's freedom.

"Oh, Käaren, Robert has not even called in six weeks. We had so much in common. The two weekends we dated were great. We both grew up in Denver and we're both attorneys. The friends who introduced us knew we would be right for each other. I was so hopeful at last a relationship would work out for me. I'm so hurt. I heard now he is dating another."

Amanda was tall, slim, brunette, and brilliant. She had ivory skin and doe-like brown eyes. Controlled and gracious—usually. At this heart-breaking moment she was fragmented and distraught.

"Think back, Amanda, how did you come across? What kind of messages did he pick up from you?" I quizzed. "What did you talk about? Did your nonverbal expressions betray you?"

"Well, I did talk about my desire for children and, well, I said I wanted them very soon. After all, I am thirty-two years old. I did invite Robert to meet my folks. Well, I guess Mother was a bit presumptuous when she said, 'Call us Mom and Dad.' Perhaps that was premature. And then I did suggest to Robert that we look at this big house that was for sale. It was near his law firm and our church."

Amanda never saw Robert again.

A few weeks later Robert made an appointment to talk with me.

"Käaren," he began, "I had been looking forward to meeting Amanda. She was a bright, warm, intelligent young lady. She came with the highest recommendations from friends. Plus I had observed her in church. I noticed she was faithful and a dedicated church worker. I appreciated her tasteful dress. She was a real lady, which seems to be rare these days. I knew another young man she had dated, a fine minister. I watched her serve others at church dinners. Her mother and father were gracious, hospitable, really loving Christian people. I was impressed with her dad's care for his wife and family and his outstanding business career."

"So as you see, I found Amanda to be somewhat of a 'dream girl,' " he continued, growing visibly more tense (he loosened his tie, which apparently was choking him!) "but something made me split. I mean, run! I have never been so enthusiastic about a young lady; she held so much promise. Yet I have never felt so panicked and trapped. And I'm a normal guy, by no means a confirmed bachelor or afraid of marriage! Don't get me wrong."

As Robert walked away, the words I told him replayed in my own head (I needed to heed them too):

Robert, we can't, we just can't violate another human being's freedom. If for one instance they sense their freedom is being violated, they are compelled to run. And never is the freedom factor more in operation than in the male-female dating scene.

People have built-in, sensitive subconscious sensors that pick up the slightest indication of freedom violation. They catch it in our eyes, in those too-fond-too-early-in-the-relationship looks or in unguarded moments in conversation, in slips that reveal we have designs and plans for the other person, I continued.

God, help me, I prayed, *never to let my imagination and fantasies grow so they threaten another. Help me to see when I am imagining more than is really there. I allow you to place the desires and motivations in some man's heart. I will trust you to bring him to me. With your power I will crush wrong, exaggerated fantasies.*

My loneliness is usually based on lies or my own selfishness.

Faith . . . from Here On

God, today I made a decision.
I will not limit you by suggesting "this guy" or "that man" for a mate.
No more will I beg, "God, arrange it! He is perfect for me!" Because faith says . . .
Don't place limits. No exact expectations.
God, I will not limit you with suggested mates, names, or lists of qualifications. (I'm burning my collections of "lists" from the past ten years.)
From today on . . .
It's *your* choice, Great God.
Never again will I limit you.
Now that adds an exciting, thrilling new dimension to faith, doesn't it?

The Gift of Singleness

"Oh, Käaren! I think I've got it!" a blond, beautifully groomed, shapely woman in her early thirties wailed as she grabbed her throat.

"Open your mouth!" I joked, yet I suspected that she had a serious concern.

"No, it's not *that*. It's singleness. I think I've got the gift of singleness," she continued shreiking.

"Let me share this with you," I began after a seminar. "I often thought through the years that perhaps I had the gift I didn't want. But God is so faithful. He provided this illustration right where I lived.

"One time I had a roommate who often said during the three years we lived together, 'You know, Käaren, I really feel as though I have the gift of singleness. I don't feel the same way as most young women our age. I don't have any interest in feathering a nest, having children or a husband. I am not longing to support a man in a marriage situation. I hate homemaking! I love the single life I have with my writing and ministering. It is for this that I long to spend my total energies. I love the gift of singleness. It is freeing!'

"She was different from my other roommates. I remember one time we were going to buy furniture together. After about three minutes of browsing, she plunked down on a sofa and said to the salesman and myself, 'I just want to read my book. You pick out what you like. I'll like it. And then I'll pay half. But please don't make me look at furniture for an hour!'

"She read her two-pound library book on the life of Winston Churchill while I savored and selected the furniture.

"I realized during those years, after careful scrutiny, that my former roommate truly had the gift of singleness. And I understood God's faithfulness.

"He would never leave a person full of desire for a mate and give them the gift of singleness. Those to whom he has given the gift know it. *They cherish it.* They thrive and soar with the prospect of singularity. And what's most important and so characteristic of God in his inimitable style and his attention to detail, he prepares them for singleness, for they see that singleness is the only way they can live out their dreams. Marriage and a family would hinder them!"

Freedom to Choose

In finding a mate, there's a balance between the will of God and my choice, my freedom.

"Käaren, about mating," Sue choked out while tugging a blazer over her 250-pound frame, "I am thirty-three years old and single. All through my twenties I kept saying, 'God hasn't brought anyone into my life. God just hasn't done it yet for me.' Well, Käaren, that goes over all through one's twenties. But into my thirties I can't fool myself anymore. I've got to take responsibility for myself. God has done his part, but I haven't done my part," she continued.

I may impress from a distance, but I only make an impact in close contact.

I can't do it all. God can. I think I'll let him.
			K.h.

I have a dream for singles: They find their dream. I don't know how close I am. I only know I'm running as fast as I can.

K.H.

"Romantic love is one of those rare human endeavors that succeeds best when it requires the least effort."

Dr. Jim Dobson
Love Must Be Tough

"Yes, there's God's will, but God gave you the freedom of choice," I interjected.

"I have chosen the wrong attitudes," she grieved. "My weight reflects a spirit of rebellion. I now realize and face it. I refused to reduce. I insisted that people had to accept me the way I am. But I'm sick of you, men, and everybody not accepting me because I am overweight!"

"Sue," I demanded, taking a tough love approach, "look, I don't care how much you weigh. I am going to love you no matter what. You are a neat, loving friend. You know that. And stop being manipulative. That's a cop-out. We've shoved that idea of acceptance, 'Accept me exactly the way I am,' down one another's throats. But sometime we must face reality, and take responsibility, and do something!"

She said she would. She is.

Foundation

What am I building on? When you're sixty-five, your company says, "You're out. We don't need you anymore. You may have built your life on us, but we didn't build our life *on you*."

Some build a life on their mate, boyfriend, child, money, youth, or beauty.

Beauty, for instance, may open doors for you for *a few* years. But then the doors close. They don't open anymore.

Rescued Again

"God, rescue me. I am crawling face down emotionally. God, please help me," I moaned, as I mindlessly moved the clothes on the store racks.

People looked up from their search for garments. I didn't care.

I had fallen into one of my life's worst emotional black holes. I was drowning. Dazed. Devastated.

Passing store windows, I caught my image. "I'm not young. I'm not a girl. I'm a woman. The clerks call me 'Ma'am' or 'Mrs. Witte.' "

Reality slaps me in the face. Easing up to a mirror for sunglasses, I see deep crow's feet.

"God, I'm over thirty. So what if I ride my bike and jog. I still am over thirty. I can't compete with younger women. What's the use? Why live through this struggle?" I continued to pray.

Eric was a fourth-year medical student. Fun. Warm. Athletic. A witnessing Christian, and a leader in the singles' group.

So why doesn't Eric ever ask me out? I question. *What do other women have that I don't?*

Why is it these old guys in their forties or even fifties call me and pursue me, I continue to complain inwardly.

Reality slaps me in the face. Eric is ten years younger than I. And what do the other women have that I don't have? Hair with no grays, firm thighs, and unlined faces, that's what.

"So Janice, what's the use of life? Why live? For what? I mean, my whole life I have been preparing for marriage! I have worked so hard to develop my skills and talents! I can host and cook a successful dinner party with the most delicious, beautifully served food. I know how to earn money, save it, and invest it. I know how to control my weight, exercise, and buy the most beautiful designer clothes *on sale!* I go to the best hair stylist in the city (and then evangelize the guy and recruit him for the singles' group!) I am a good daughter and have a precious relationship with my folks. I have sacrificed to make my life count—building the kingdom, sharing the gospel, traveling the world and writing books. And all the years on the road! All so I could be 'the woman behind the man.' And it is all for nothing," I cried to a friend on the phone.

"Käaren, you're giving me double messages," Jan confronted.

"Janice, if someone called me to speak at the biggest conference in the country right now, I would say, 'I don't have a message,' " I answered, broken and crying.

Janice said two things.

"Käaren, if you were married, you would be giving me the same emotional song and dance about life—only your husband would be in the other room, probably shaking his head in frustration. Life gets fulfilled in the process. You weren't accomplishing all those wonderful things just in preparation for marriage.

"And another thing. You have dreamed, planned, pined, and fantasized about marriage since you were a little girl."

"Oh yes, I have planned and dreamed since I was four! I began cutting out wedding dresses from *Bride's* magazine when I was eleven. I made a scrapbook of my future dream house, collected hundreds of recipes, and embroidered linens," I added.

"But Käaren, you've put your total life, your hopes and dreams, into your future mate. Maybe the man will die or become a quadriplegic. Then what?"

She's right, I thought. I admitted it to her.

"Käaren, dear Käaren. A mate is wonderful, of course. But a mate is a mate is a mate! Get it in perspective for what it is. He's a man—*not* God," Janice concluded.

She didn't say any more. Once again I was free, balanced. My head was on straight, my mate in perspective.

The light went on. I was rescued, one more time.

My Friend had heard my deep cries from the dress department of Miss Jackson's store.

Not Flawless, But Perfect

Dan and Ann got engaged today.

When Dan first came to church I talked with him for three hours. He was twenty-seven and desired to find a special young lady.

"Käaren, you'd love him if you knew him like I do," Fred said, regarding another person who I thought was impossible to love.

Know a person. Know all about him or her.

That's the answer.

K↲

I tried to determine what was important to him. Finally I said, "Have you met Ann?" He had just met her.

I told Dan that she was an excellent young lady—hard working, consistent, sincere, moral, giving, fun, and talented.

Eight months later they got engaged. I love how Dan evaluated mating. It applies to many life situations: "Our relationship isn't flawless, but it's perfect."

My Ego

This is my ego's and security's bottom line:
What God has done.
Who God is.
Nothing else
matters.

Assurance

Some moments I hear, *Käaren, look what you have in life: not much. You are well into your thirties now. You don't have a wonderful, successful husband and beautiful, healthy children with manners that charm teachers and neighbors. You don't even own a condo. Baby, this is mid-life. Face it. You didn't get what you wanted the most in the world, did you? Arms to hold you. A husband to cherish and nurture you. A man for you to believe in, encourage, and watch achieve. And other people to speak about you as 'chosen by God to be the wife of . . .'—voices that speak with awe and honor of the chosen.*

The women who get married. I question around and around in my head. *The wives—they were chosen. Yet are they more caring, talented, well groomed than I? Why were they chosen by quality men, men of world-leader caliber?*

I am riddled with self-doubt. *Face it. You don't have it. You can't see it, but something's missing.*

But then I petition Father God on my own behalf. It is granted—my assurance.

This is me, sometimes, in the moments nobody sees. I refuse to place myself among the gaggle of speakers and writers who paint a phony picture of the Christian life. One lives a tough life when one chooses to follow the awesome Jesus Christ.

What has it cost me to follow Jesus Christ?

Everything.

Still I would say, "I give you my life. I serve you. I work each day to bring some glory to your name and further your kingdom."

In the moments when the lies scream, I hold my head and scream back, "NO! I don't want to grab for the wind with my days, my time, my life. I am building for eternity. I have lived and invested in the richest part of life, in that which cannot be stolen, that which doesn't die. I have lived and gained in the invisible."

The best, richest part of life is always lived in the invisible.

The best things in life are not things.

Awe and Wonder

I want my sense of wonder and awe of God to be so alive. I want to sense his "divine mystery."

So many are bored with God.

I don't ever want to lack the personal thrill of believing God is preparing, planning, arranging, connecting, working in others' hearts and minds, and supernaturally pulling for me.

I want to be real. Not religious.

Fall 1984

Not Too Seriously

"I wish people wouldn't take dating so seriously," one young man told me. "I would love to take out more girls. I like to spend time with a lot of different people. But they take it too seriously, and that spoils all the fun."

People are more fascinating than clothes, houses, cars, decorating, crafts, or travel. I like an evening where I leave and think, "We simply got a better understanding of each other." No psychoanalyzing. No in-depth therapy. Just warmth, appreciation, and concern.

How beautiful . . . if we could all just relax and remember the purpose for dating.

A Buddy . . . Please, Jesus

"Diane, I don't want to go to Israel," I confided the night before I would fly to New York to connect with that long El-Al flight to Tel Aviv. "I just won't have a good buddy. You know, one friend with whom I'll experience it. One friend to help. One friend I'll pull for. If ever life requires a team effort, it's in international travel. You need to bond together. You're so far from home and anything or anybody familiar. Well, I just need somebody in my tour group to be there to pull the right lens out of my backpack. A pal to buy a piece of fruit for a snack and share it. A friend to lean over and yell, 'Look at that! See the Bedouin tents and the women wearing ancient chadors!'

"Oh, I know a lot of the people going on the trip, but they all know each other and are friends. I just don't see a good buddy for me," I continued, resigning myself. "But that's life. No one will know my need. I'll just suppress it and be everybody's friend, like always."

"Käaren, I'm going to pray. I'm going to carry the faith.

You borrow from my faith for this one. I lend you my hope, okay?" Diane comforted.

"Okay," I answered. (But I thought, *Easy for you to say.*)

"Dear God, before Käaren leaves for this study-tour with the group, I pray for a good buddy for her. A buddy with whom she may share her heart and life. A buddy who will see her worth, and of course, one to laugh with!"

Within two days of travel, something in Kristi's spirit hit mine. We were soul mates. In Tulsa, we had been only casual aquaintances. But now we were destined to be together. World significance stuff. So much so that we kept gasping, "I can't wait to see what the Lord is going to do next!"

Kristi: Single. Early thirties. A world citizen. Adorable looking and acting. Bright. A comrade. A confidante. An unparalleled ability to see the little ludicrous and absurd happenings in life, and to laugh. A buddy.

Jogging Around Galilee

Israel.
Today I ran where Jesus walked.

Contagious Attitudes

Within a few days of returning from Israel, Kristi and I were playing racquetball.

Kristi was a little better than I. We were both fiercely competitive. Nikes squealing, we were running. Sweating. Slamming the ball. Stretching screaming muscles. Banging rackets on the floor and wall.

I'd be trailing her by a few points, then we would tie. Then I would soar ahead a few points.

At one long volley I lagged several points. We forgot the exact score, but we both knew Kristi was ahead.

"Aw, let's just call it fourteen even," Kristi yelled to me as I served.

No easy sacrifice for a competitive athlete like her, I thought, moved by her attitude.

"I added it up. I owe you seventy-five dollars for money I borrowed on the trip," Kristi announced later in the locker room.

"Ah. Um, let's just call it . . . 'fourteen even.' " I smiled.
She smiled.
She knew.

Confessing One to Another

Something happened to me in Israel. Something painful. I saw myself. The false, phony me. I can't say for sure what triggered it.

"Jesus, forgive me. I've failed you. I've failed my listeners, readers, and everyone," I cried the day after our close-knit group returned to the United States, in the aloneness of unpacking and the jetlag misery of waking up at 3:00 A.M., in the strangeness of being severed from my travel "family" to whom I had become "blood." (Goodness, we had become bonded, crying together at Jesus' tomb and singing "Up from the Grave He Arose!" Laughing at the ludicrous bargaining going on in the Old City section of Jerusalem. Protesting and pulling for one another half a world away.) Now, a new horror.

"Diane," I wept to my Tulsa friend, "I began to think about my motives while in the Middle East. I have suppressed them artfully all my adult life. But today the burden exploded.

"All my adult life I have had three motivations for everything I've done: Be successful (be a somebody); be acceptable to other people; be attractive to the opposite sex, to attract and secure a quality husband. I think of the money I spent on clothes, health and beauty aids, trips, cars, furnishings, staying fit and healthy, education, jewelry—why? The lovely apartment, the furnishings, the hospitality, the beautiful dinners and parties—why? Was it to further the kingdom of my great, redeeming Christ? No.

"I always silence these gnawing haunts with, 'I'm dressing to please Christ! I must look like the King's kid. I'm jogging for Jesus! I'm living in prosperity so everyone will say it is Christ! Then they too will worship him!' " I continued.

"Diane, today I fell to my knees, as I have every morning. But I was changed—new, real, whole, pure," I concluded.

"Jesus Christ, forgive me. Forgive me for using you and my ministry to get what I wanted. Forgive my motives. They were wrong. I wanted to further Käaren Witte more than you," I had prayed on that turning-point morning of my life.

Later that day I was in a department store. Old habit patterns and thoughts die hard, slow, excruciating deaths.

Cruising through the cosmetics and clothing departments, I heard my familiar thoughts: *What will make me more appealing, attractive, eyecatching, alluring?* I still wasn't initially thinking, *Jesus, what will glorify you and further your kingdom?*

The old Käaren Witte dies slowly. But it will, because I want it to. At last.

The little saying I have hanging on my living room wall revolves in my head: "When all is said and done and bought and used and worn, the only thing that really matters is Jesus Christ."

New Year's Eve 1984

Memories

I feel the passage of time deeply at this stage of my life. My emotions are captured and crystallized this New Year's Eve.

I remember my dad tickling my tummy when I was little. My mom kissing my sticky mouth and laughing.

I remember my dad kissing my cheek in the night, before he went to bed. I would wake up but not open my eyes.

The memories. Mom and Dad praying one evening in the family room. I was a teen, listening at the door. Mom whispered Dad's name. He whispered hers. They thanked God for each other.

Dad reminisced, "Thank you, God, for our babies. We were so young. With you we made it work."

I didn't store memories consciously. Little did I know they would carry me for a lifetime.

Memories. Sometime later I'll come here again.

God,
I bless you for the ministry of laughter.

    K.H.

Good looks and attractiveness and beauty consist of two things: good health and good grooming, inside and outside.

KH

Another Prayer

God, when we trust you, the odds are always against us. Have you noticed?

Take Noah. You asked him to build an ark for a flood. And I know you remember, there never had been such a flood.

Take my role model and heroine, Sarah. You said she was going to have a child at ninety.

However, dear God, through the years I have found that if I can "work it out," it's not a test of faith.

I have learned faith may not give me a child or mate when I so desire, but it will enable me to hang on. To endure. To wait patiently, in the face of insurmountable odds and statistics.

I know you are ready to use the person with faith. She's your advertisement, your object lesson.

I love the assignments you've given me. They are impossible situations. And others know it!

I feed on the impossible. I consider what the God of heaven—the God with the 100 percent perfect track record in my life—is able to pull off.

I will see things from your perspective, God: Nothing is impossible.

Most of all, help the singles at church and around the world to catch the fire and faith that are in my heart. Amen.

Just Joking

A talk-show host asked me, "Do you think your husband (when you get married) should share the responsibilities for the house also? How about the cooking?"

"Sure," I quipped, "he can phone for a pizza as well as I can."

"Well, are you practicing cooking during your single days?" he continued to probe.

"While grocery shopping, I go to the shelves with boxes

We don't need others to tell us what we are lacking and what's wrong with us. We know better than they do.

that say 'Just add water' and I throw them into the cart," I clowned. "But I don't squeeze the vegetables yet."

One single man was bragging about some single young lady: "Wow, can she cook."

"Big deal," I said and smiled. "I can thaw."

Looking Back, Laughing Helps

I remember one guy I dated (briefly).

I had purchased two tickets for the ballet. (Thirty-five bucks each—sorry, depression-raised, dear Dad.) I didn't expect this date to be thrilled, but I thought it would increase his cultural awareness. Plus I wanted someone to go with me.

"Surprise! I have two tickets to the Russian ballet!" I exclaimed when he arrived to collect me for dinner.

"What? Russian ballet? I don't want to see a bunch of Commie fruits leapin' around without their pants on," he roared, then burst into uncontrollable gales of laughter. No, patrons of the arts, all men are not created equal.

Another guy I dated (briefly) hailed from California. He insisted on having a stock Hollywood tan all year.

"You're not considered legally dead 'til your tan fades," he'd assure me.

"I want to take your picture," I said one day whole he was helping me wash the car.

"I only have my pictures taken 'on location,' " he answered. (He was serious.)

Choices

Choices, sometimes painful and crushing. Choices, gambling on eternity.

I made a choice never to be upset with God because he has not given me a mate. For if I hadn't made that choice, I might never have overcome temptations.

Often we have the idea, "I deserve this pleasure because I've been shortchanged," and that causes us to give up the struggle.

God has a right to do as he wishes with his own. And unless we accept that we will fail in our struggle against sin.

The clay submits to the potter.

I accept God's will for me. Singleness is from his hand. When I accept his will, I'm in a better position to say no to temptation. And yes to him.

I am willing to walk through the landmines to pave the way for other sister and brother singles.

I won't defect. I owe the singles around the world so much. They have loved me, supported me, and trusted me.

A girl named Elizabeth, a fifth grade schoolteacher from a little town in east Texas, worked her way through the crowd after a conference. She told me how she had prayed for a mate.

"Pray and prepare, sweet girl," I encouraged.

Her arms pressed around my shoulders. She clung. I held on to her too. She cried wordlessly. I cried, but I didn't want to weep as much as she did.

But I did.

Somehow as a speaker and writer I wanted to appear stronger and more courageous than anyone in my audiences.

But maybe people have loved me and nurtured me because they knew and sensed behind my persona of author, speaker, and television personality that I was spiritually, emotionally fragile. And I needed them.

Years have passed since my encounter with Elizabeth.

Hundreds of Elizabeths have cried with me. But more than that, I've covenanted with them all to trust our incredible Christ more. Further. No deadlines. Just for a lifetime.

I'm committed to serve God. I'm committed to marry only God's man. I covenant today with you. And you with me.

A Secret

"Käaren, you carry a secret in your heart. I see it. Does love really, I mean *really*, exist?" a single, twenty-nine-year-old, shy, sweet, never-married surgical nurse questioned me. "Do you really believe in love, Käaren?"

"Dear friend," I confirmed, "there is a great love. My soul is satisfied. A great all-consuming purpose for living and dreaming and being. There is such a love. A thousand times warmer and more fulfilling than the one I had longed for before."

It is Christ, my soul to his soul. Joy waves hello. Peace smiles back. Hope lives. No disappointments. And how is it that he loves me? I can't understand. The cross hides my past.

My soul. Created for him. My soul. It sings. It sings, "It is well."

At last.

Fall 1985

The Promised Land!

(Good-bye Quiche, Hello Knish)

I left my heart in the Middle East.
Not to worry.
Psalm 37:34 loosely translated: "Have I got a deal for you!" (All due respect to King David.)
After fourteen years in singles' ministries, a new role awaits me, half a world away.
On November 2, 1985, God willing, I'll fly to Jerusalem and be based there for an indefinite period while speaking, writing, and studying.
It's amazing. I've been groomed for this new phase of life. I'm in awe of God's attention to detail (necessary to pull this move off). God has created the perfect background for me.
I've known a lifetime of good-byes, living and growing up in a mobile family. My background includes extensive international travel and experience in living in different cultures.
My other preparation has included learning submission and servanthood (continual goals), running a ministry, and learning personal financial management. Most of all, I have learned that the ministry of Jesus Christ is the only thing that really matters in this life. I have discovered the emptiness and loneliness in striving for recognition, in trying to be "somebody."
I have learned to be self-sufficient. (This by no means

indicates I'm a women's libber! Yes, I'd love for you to carry my boxes.)

I have learned to overcome opposition! Before every major move for God I was forced to make a difficult choice.

One month before leaving for Korea as a short-term missionary, I was offered a media job by one of the most influential men in television.

The day I started as a singles' director I was contacted for a journalism job with a starting salary four times higher!

My interest in missions goes back to my early childhood. When I first learned to print, my mom encouraged me to correspond with missionaries. (In basic letters on my Big Chief tablet with a fat pencil and/or crayola.)

Again, most of all I remember hearing my parents praying on their knees before dawn, "Help our daughter develop a heart and life bent toward ministry. God, create a precious, submissive, gentle spirit, a servant, and a godly young woman. We know you will guide her in her choices of ministry and mate. God, give her wisdom and let us influence her for greatness, for your glory. We cooperate with you in the plan for our dear girl."

With that kind of love, sacrifice, and commitment, I owed it to them to make wise choices. But I confess. I have doubted God in the darkness. I know what it is to fall into emotional black holes and cry in the night, "God, are you going to do anything more with my life? Are you? Or did I blow it with you, and we're through?"

God was faithfully preparing and arranging. He poured on the grace.

So this year, in some of my most desolate moments, in the winters of my soul, I trusted a little further. My hand in his. Eyes closed.

So now I know what it is to be rescued while under heavy, dark clouds of emotion that won't blow away. Intermittently bittersweet.

All the time he was arranging with his supernatural network, even when my heart stumbled and fell, leaving me feeling exposed and vulnerable as never before in my life. How I wish I had never doubted him!

Postscript

Dear Readers,

So many of you have written. Thank you for sharing your hearts with me and saying, "I know how you feel."

We must remember that any isolation or emptiness we feel in life involves more than our relationships with our boyfriends, girlfriends, wives, or husbands. That's just scratching the surface.

We must then ask great questions. Serious questions. Why am I working or going to school? Why did I get married or remain single? Our answer as followers of Christ must be, "No matter what I am doing or where I am, all my actions and goals are to further the kingdom."

I love hearing from my readers, and I answer my mail! You may write to me in care of Abingdon Press, 201 Eighth Avenue South, P.O. Box 801, Nashville, Tennessee 37202.

May you be satisfied with the good things of the Lord and stand on my shoulders. Reach higher than I. And remember, after all is said and done, please remember me for only one thing—loving you.

                      Love always, I promise,

                      Käaren Witte

Your church, singles' group, or conference can sponsor a seminar on successful singularity with such topics as "How to Find Your Master, Ministry, and Mate (And in That Order!)," "How to Kill a Relationship Without Being Accused of Murder!" and "Hello, Wall." Write Käaren Witte, care of Abingdon Press, 201 Eighth Avenue South, P.O. Box 801, Nashville, TN 37202.

Additional Topics:

How to Get Married and Stay Married

Beating the System (The Dating System)

How to Avoid Indiscriminate Relationships

How to Judge the Character of a Man and Woman

Single Self-Talk

How to Cope with Not Dating, Not Mating, and Just Plain Waiting

What Men Wish Single Women Knew

Blind Spots and Bitter Roots

A Miss, Mess, or Mesh?